EYEWITNESS

THE ELEMENTS

Written by
ADRIAN DINGLE

Flakes of pure gold refined in a laboratory

Stalactites made of deposits of calcium carbonate

DK | Penguin Random House

REVISED EDITION

DK DELHI
Senior Editor Virien Chopra **Senior Art Editor** Vikas Chauhan
DTP Designer Pawan Kumar **Picture Researcher** Vishal Ghavri
Managing Editor Kingshuk Ghoshal **Managing Art Editor** Govind Mittal
Jacket Designer Gayatri Menon
Senior Jackets Coordinator Priyanka Sharma Saddi

DK LONDON
Editor Kelsie Besaw **Art Editor** Chrissy Barnard
US Editor Heather Wilcox **US Executive Editor** Lori Cates Hand
Managing Editor Francesca Baines **Managing Art Editor** Philip Letsu
Production Editor Jacqueline Street-Elkayam
Senior Production Controller Jude Crozier
Jacket Design Development Manager Sophia MTT
Publisher Andrew Macintyre
Associate Publishing Director Liz Wheeler
Art Director Karen Self
Publishing Director Jonathan Metcalf

Consultant Kat Day

FIRST EDITION

DK DELHI
Senior editor Rupa Rao **Project art editor** Pooja Pipil
Editor Charvi Arora **Art editors** Mansi Agrawal, Priyanka Bansal
Jacket designer Juhi Sheth **Jackets editorial coordinator** Priyanka Sharma
Senior DTP designer Harish Aggarwal
DTP designers Pawan Kumar, Syed Md Farhan, Vikram Singh
Managing jackets editor Saloni Singh
Managing editor Kingshuk Ghoshal **Managing art editor** Govind Mittal

DK LONDON
Senior editor Ashwin Khurana **Senior art editor** Spencer Holbrook
Picture researcher Liz Moore
Jacket designer Surabhi Wadhwa-Gandhi
Jacket editor Claire Gell
Jacket design development manager Sophia MTT
Producer, pre-production Andy Hilliard
Senior producer Angela Graef
Managing editor Francesca Baines
Managing art editor Philip Letsu
Publisher Andrew Macintyre
Associate publishing director Liz Wheeler
Art director Karen Self
Design director Phil Ormerod
Publishing director Jonathan Metcalf

Written by Adrian Dingle
Consultant: John Gillespie, M Sc

This Eyewitness ® Book has been conceived
by Dorling Kindersley Limited and Editions Gallimard

This American Edition, 2022
First American Edition, 2018
Published in the United States by DK Publishing
1745 Broadway, 20th Floor, New York, NY 10019

Copyright © 2018, 2022 Dorling Kindersley Limited
DK, a Division of Penguin Random House LLC
22 23 24 25 26 10 9 8 7 6 5 4 3 2 1
001–335495–Dec/2022

A catalog record for this book
is available from the Library of Congress.
ISBN 978-0-7440-7983-8 (Paperback)
ISBN 978-0-7440-7984-5 (ALB)

DK books are available at special discounts when purchased
in bulk for sales promotions, premiums, fund-raising, or
educational use. For details, contact: DK Publishing Special Markets,
1745 Broadway, 20th Floor, New York, NY 10019
SpecialSales@dk.com

Printed and bound in China

For the curious
www.dk.com

Pure iodine stored in a glass sphere

The Eiffel Tower, Paris, France, made of wrought iron

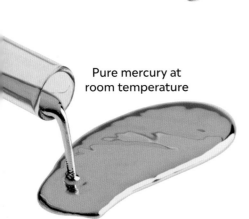

Copper wire

Pure mercury at room temperature

Contents

What is an element?

An element is a substance that cannot be broken down into simpler ingredients. Each one is made up of building blocks called atoms, which are unique for every element. For example, the element carbon contains only carbon atoms. There are 118 elements, and most, such as oxygen and gold, are found naturally on Earth—although rarely in their pure state. Elements are vital to our everyday lives, from the aluminum used to make kitchen foil to the zinc in our muscles and bones.

Liquid mercury at room temperature

Solid crystals of pure strontium refined in a laboratory

Elemental forms

All the elements exist in one of three primary states under normal conditions of temperature and pressure. They are either a solid, a liquid, or a gas, although a fourth special state called plasma is sometimes seen. At room temperature, most elements are solids. Only a few are gases, and only mercury and bromine are liquids.

States of matter

Elements can exist in three states: solid, liquid, and gas. An element can change from one state to another. For example, solid gallium can melt into a liquid, while liquid bromine can evaporate into a gas. The changes do not alter the atoms of the element but arrange them in a more, or less, rigid way.

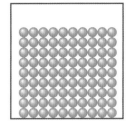

Solid
In solids, the atoms are attracted to one another, are arranged in a regular pattern, and have little energy to move around.

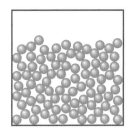

Liquid
As solids become liquids, the attraction between the atoms weakens. They have no fixed arrangement and more energy.

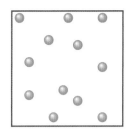

Gas
As liquids become gases, the atoms are very weakly attracted to each other. They spread out as far as possible and have a lot of energy.

Raw forms

Elements are commonly found in one of two ways. If they are unreactive and do not easily combine with other elements, they may be found in their pure state, such as gold. Elements that are more reactive always combine with other elements around them. This combination is called a compound.

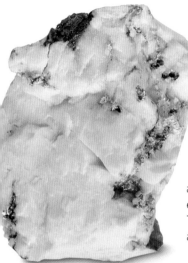

Gold in quartz

Compounds

When elements chemically bond with one another in a fixed ratio, they form compounds. For example, in sodium chloride, sodium combines with chlorine in an equal ratio to form a compound. Water is a compound formed when two hydrogen atoms combine with one oxygen atom to make one molecule.

Common salt
(sodium chloride)

Pure hydrogen gas in a glass sphere

Mixtures

When elements or compounds combine in an unequal ratio without chemically bonding with one another, the resulting combination is called a mixture. Mixtures can be easily separated. For example, the combination of lather and food coloring seen on the right is a mixture that can be separated by filtering.

The human body

About 99 percent of the human body is made from just six elements: oxygen, carbon, hydrogen, nitrogen, calcium, and phosphorus. They combine together to form thousands of different compounds. More than 60 percent of the body is water, but there are about 25 elements that are required to make our bodies work properly. They are called the "essential elements."

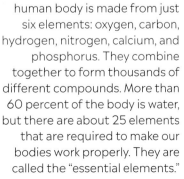

Phosphorus 1%   Others 1%

Calcium 1.5%   Nitrogen 3%

Hydrogen 10%

Carbon 18.5%

Oxygen 65%

Inside an **atom**

Everything we see around us is made of very small particles called atoms. Atoms are so tiny that they cannot be observed with the naked eye. They are the smallest units of any element, but the atoms themselves are made up of even smaller "subatomic" particles called protons, electrons, and neutrons. The number of protons in an atom of an element is unique to that element.

Electrons travel around the nucleus in three-dimensional areas of space called orbitals.

The dense nucleus at the center of the atom is where nearly all the mass of an atom lies.

Subatomic particles

Protons and neutrons are found in the core, or nucleus, at the center of the atom, while electrons orbit the nucleus. Protons and electrons have exactly equal but opposite charges; protons are positive, and electrons are negative. Neutrons carry no charge. Because atoms have an equal number of protons and electrons, and neutrons contribute no charge, atoms in their natural state are neutral. Protons and neutrons have the same mass, while electrons are about 10,000 times smaller.

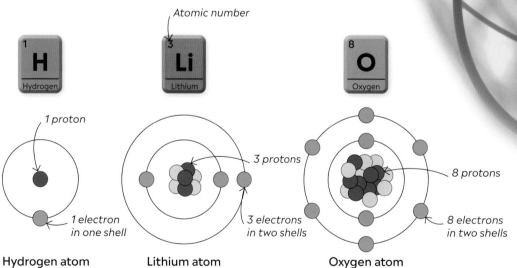

Atomic number

1		3		8
H		Li		O
Hydrogen		Lithium		Oxygen

1 proton

1 electron in one shell

3 protons

3 electrons in two shells

8 protons

8 electrons in two shells

Hydrogen atom   Lithium atom   Oxygen atom

The orbitals are arranged around the nucleus, at various distances, in layers called shells.

What is the atomic number?

The atomic number of an element tells us how many protons are found inside the nucleus of a single atom of that element. For example, a lithium atom (above) has three protons in its nucleus, which means its atomic number is 3. The elements are arranged on the periodic table in the increasing order of their atomic number, starting with hydrogen, the simplest element, with just one proton.

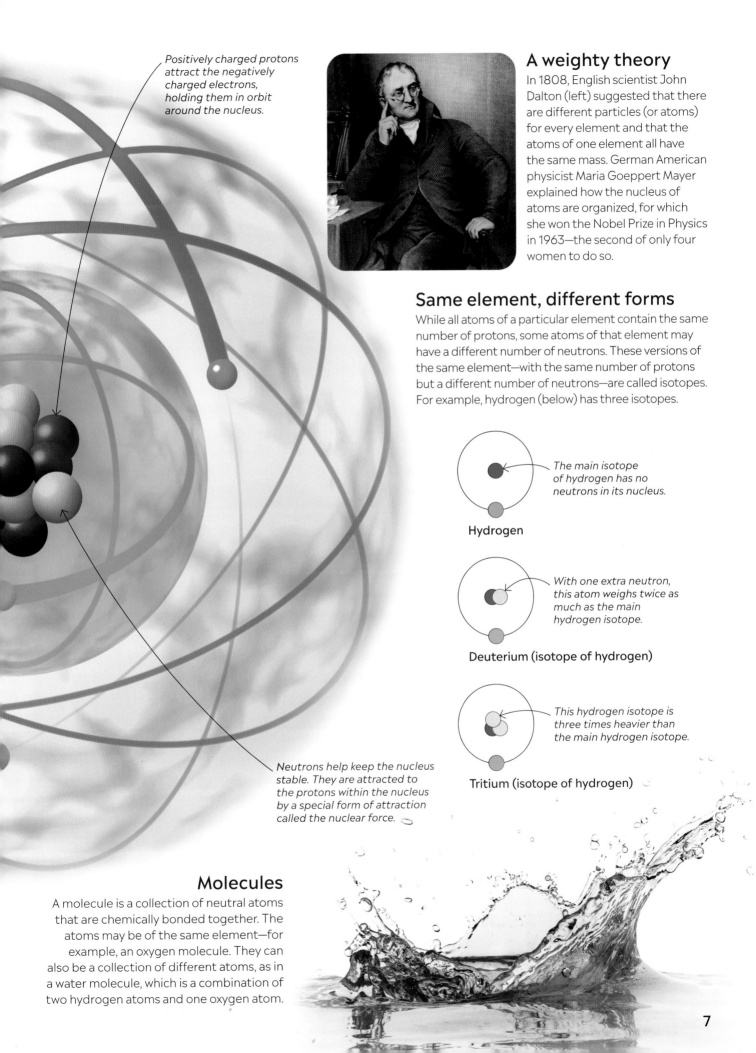

Positively charged protons attract the negatively charged electrons, holding them in orbit around the nucleus.

A weighty theory

In 1808, English scientist John Dalton (left) suggested that there are different particles (or atoms) for every element and that the atoms of one element all have the same mass. German American physicist Maria Goeppert Mayer explained how the nucleus of atoms are organized, for which she won the Nobel Prize in Physics in 1963—the second of only four women to do so.

Same element, different forms

While all atoms of a particular element contain the same number of protons, some atoms of that element may have a different number of neutrons. These versions of the same element—with the same number of protons but a different number of neutrons—are called isotopes. For example, hydrogen (below) has three isotopes.

The main isotope of hydrogen has no neutrons in its nucleus.

Hydrogen

With one extra neutron, this atom weighs twice as much as the main hydrogen isotope.

Deuterium (isotope of hydrogen)

This hydrogen isotope is three times heavier than the main hydrogen isotope.

Tritium (isotope of hydrogen)

Neutrons help keep the nucleus stable. They are attracted to the protons within the nucleus by a special form of attraction called the nuclear force.

Molecules

A molecule is a collection of neutral atoms that are chemically bonded together. The atoms may be of the same element—for example, an oxygen molecule. They can also be a collection of different atoms, as in a water molecule, which is a combination of two hydrogen atoms and one oxygen atom.

The periodic table

Many scientists had tried to arrange the known elements into an organized list long before Russian chemist Dmitri Mendeleev produced his first table of elements in 1869. Mendeleev's table was periodic, or repeating, because the characteristics of elements followed a pattern. It was the forerunner to the modern periodic table.

Reading the table

The periodic table is made up of a series of groups (columns that run from top to bottom), and periods (rows that run from left to right).

Groups

Elements in the same group have the same number of electrons in their outermost shell. As you move down a group, the atoms of the elements get larger and heavier. This is because there is an increasing number of protons in the nucleus and more electrons in shells around the nucleus.

One shell

Hydrogen
An atom of hydrogen has one electron in total.

Two shells

Lithium
A lithium atom has three electrons in total, with one in its outer shell.

Three shells

Sodium
A sodium atom has eleven electrons in total, with one in its outer shell.

Groups
A vertical column of chemically similar elements is known as a group.

Periods
A horizontal row of chemically different elements is known as a period.

Lanthanides and actinides
The "f" block elements are sometimes called the inner transition metals.

KEY

- Hydrogen
- Alkali Metals
- Alkaline Earth Metals
- Transition Metals
- Lanthanides
- Actinides
- The Boron Group
- The Carbon Group
- The Nitrogen Group
- The Oxygen Group
- Halogens
- Noble Gases

Groups (columns)

Periods (rows)

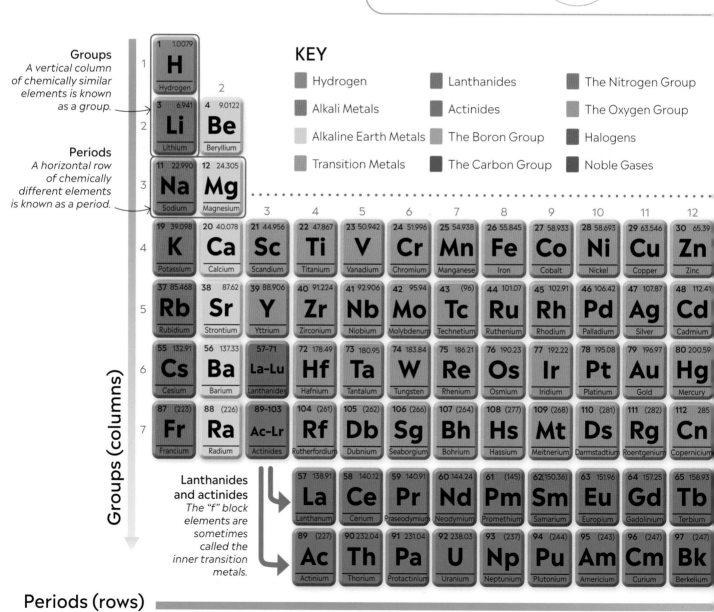

Periods

As you move across a period, the atoms of each element have the same number of shells. However, as you move across the period, the number of electrons in the outer shell increases. In the examples below, each element has three shells. The different numbers of electrons in the outer shells mean that these elements have differences in their chemical properties.

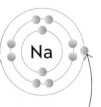

One electron

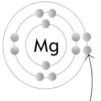

Two electrons

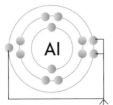

Three electrons

Sodium
A sodium atom has eleven electrons in total, with one in its outer shell.

Magnesium
A magnesium atom has twelve electrons in total, with two in its outer shell.

Aluminum
An aluminum atom has thirteen electrons in total, with three in its outer shell.

Blocks

Within the periodic table there are larger collections of elements known as blocks. Three of these blocks—the "s" block, the "d" block, and the "f" block—contain elements that have many broad similarities with one another, but the "p" block contains a much more diverse set of elements.

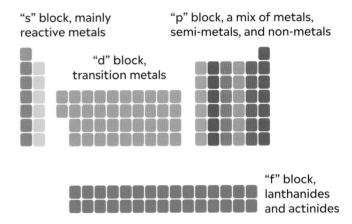

"s" block, mainly reactive metals

"d" block, transition metals

"p" block, a mix of metals, semi-metals, and non-metals

"f" block, lanthanides and actinides

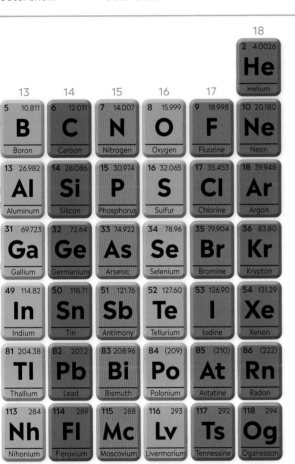

Elemental information

Each element is given a tile with important information to identify it. These include the element's name, symbol, atomic number, and atomic mass number.

Atomic number
This is the number of protons in the nucleus of an atom of an element. A beryllium atom has four protons in its nucleus, so its atomic number is four.

Atomic mass number
This number shows the average mass of the atoms of all the naturally occurring forms (isotopes) of a given element. Beryllium has 12 known isotopes, and their average mass is 9.0122 AMU (atomic mass units).

Name
The elements are named after people, places, their sources, and many other things.

Chemical symbol
Each element is given either a one- or two-letter symbol. This is the shortened version of the element's English or Latin name. The first letter is always uppercase, and when there are two letters, the second is always lowercase.

Dmitri Mendeleev

The Russian scientist Mendeleev is usually thought of as the pioneer of the modern periodic table. His original arrangement organized the elements by atomic mass and also left gaps that accurately predicted the existence of some unknown elements, which would be discovered later.

Elemental groups and **sets**

Within the periodic table, elements are divided into smaller groups and sets that often have similar chemical properties or are related to one another in some other way.

Hydrogen

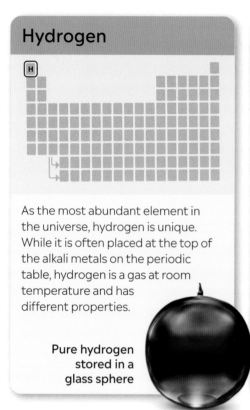

As the most abundant element in the universe, hydrogen is unique. While it is often placed at the top of the alkali metals on the periodic table, hydrogen is a gas at room temperature and has different properties.

Pure hydrogen stored in a glass sphere

Alkali Metals

The alkali metals generally have low densities, are soft enough to be cut with a knife, and react violently with both water and air. As a result, they are often stored under a protective layer of oil or in an airless container.

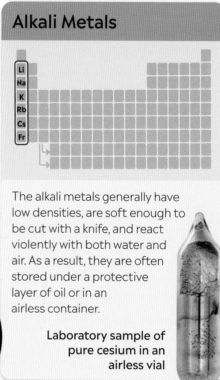

Laboratory sample of pure cesium in an airless vial

Alkaline Earth Metals

A little less reactive than their group one neighbors, these get their name from the fact that most of them were discovered as oxide compounds in Earth.

Crystals of pure calcium refined in a laboratory

Transition Metals

These metals form the largest set of elements in the periodic table. They share many properties with each other, such as their ability to form colored compounds, and are often used in specialized alloys.

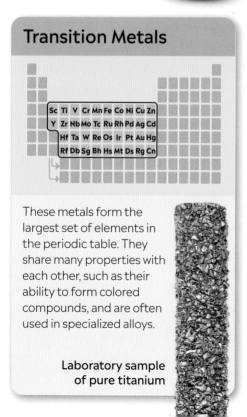

Laboratory sample of pure titanium

Lanthanides

Although they were once known as the "rare earths," the elements in this set are not rare at all. The idea of rarity came from the fact that they are difficult to separate from one another, so they were difficult to find.

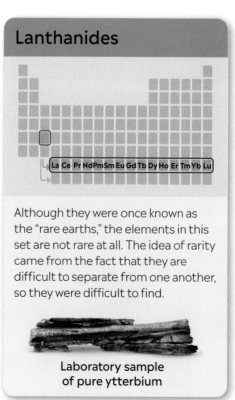

Laboratory sample of pure ytterbium

Actinides

Mostly radioactive, actinides are not found commonly in nature, with a few exceptions. Many of them are only produced artificially and have little use beyond research, although uranium is used as fuel in nuclear power plants.

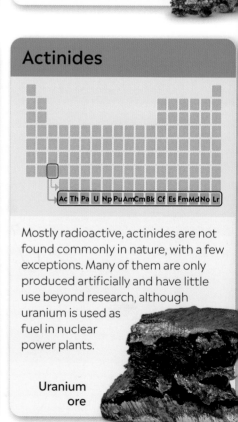

Uranium ore

The Boron Group

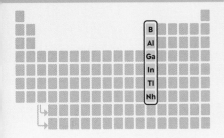

Although none of these elements are very reactive, they do differ in other ways. Aluminum is hard and has many uses, including in construction; gallium melts at just 86°F (30°C); and thallium is poisonous.

Pellets of pure aluminum refined in a laboratory

The Carbon Group

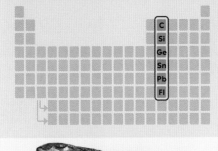

Laboratory sample of pure tin

Group 14 includes the non-metal carbon, the semi-metals silicon and germanium, the metals tin and lead, and unstable, radioactive flerovium—the newest member of the group.

The Nitrogen Group

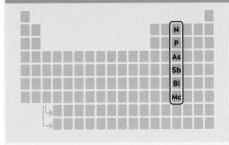

Non-metals, semi-metals, and metals make up the nitrogen group. Nitrogen is a gas at room temperature, while the others are solids. Moscovium—an artificial element—is not yet well understood.

Bismuth crystals refined in a laboratory

The Oxygen Group

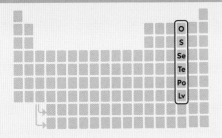

The elements in group 16 are diverse. There are two non-metals (oxygen and sulfur), three semi-metals (selenium, tellurium, and polonium), and livermorium, which is a relatively new element.

Chunk of pure selenium refined in a laboratory

Halogens

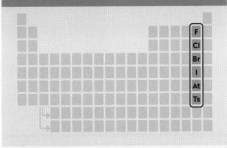

The word *halogen* means "salt forming" because the group 17 elements readily form salts when they react with metals. It contains fluorine, chlorine, bromine, iodine, astatine, and tennessine.

Liquid bromine (bottom) and bromine gas in a glass sphere

Noble Gases

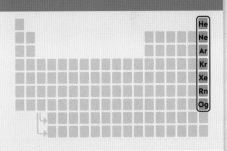

Colorless, odorless, and tasteless, the group 18 elements are not very reactive. Their reluctance to react with the other elements led to their being called "noble"—the same way that rulers do not interact with their subjects.

Pure argon glowing in response to an electric discharge

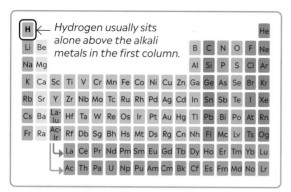

Hydrogen usually sits alone above the alkali metals in the first column.

Hydrogen

H 1

The first member of the periodic table, hydrogen is the simplest and lightest of all the elements. Although it is the most abundant element in the universe, you cannot smell, taste, or see hydrogen. In stars and "gas giant" planets, such as Jupiter, it is present mainly as a gas, while on Earth, it is present as part of water. For humans, hydrogen has many uses, from fertilizers to green fuel.

Colorless, pure hydrogen gas is stored inside this glass sphere and gives off a purple glow when electrified.

Life-giver

Water is vital to life on Earth. A single molecule of water contains two atoms of hydrogen and one atom of oxygen. Earth's surface is made up of 71 percent water, in the form of oceans and lakes, which is where most of the world's hydrogen is found.

Clouds in space

Hydrogen is abundant in the Orion Nebula, which is a dense cloud of hot gases and dust in space. Within these clouds of gas, new stars are born when hydrogen and other gases contract under the pressure of gravity. This nebula is located 1,300 light-years away from Earth, meaning it takes 1,300 years for light to reach us from this cosmic cloud.

Powering the Sun

The sun is a massive ball of flaming hydrogen and helium. The source of the sun's energy is its hot, dense core, where hydrogen atoms undergo a process of fusion to produce the gas helium. More than 661 tons of hydrogen are converted into helium each second, releasing intense heat and light.

The sun is about 75 percent hydrogen.

Hydrogen-powered bus in Japan

ROCKET FUEL

Some space rockets are powered by liquid hydrogen. This element combines with liquid oxygen to create extremely hot steam, which escapes out of the nozzle with great force. This produces a thrust that pushes the rocket upward. As an added benefit, this process generates only steam as a by-product, making hydrogen an environmentally safe choice of fuel.

1. This chamber contains liquid hydrogen.

2. This chamber contains liquid oxygen.

3. Pumps control the flow of the liquids as they enter the combustion chamber.

4. The combustion chamber is where the liquids come together, creating an explosive mixture that is ignited to create hot steam.

5. The explosive mixture passes through the nozzle, creating steam that pushes the rocket upward.

Clean fuel

Pure hydrogen is a clean energy source and is used to power some vehicles. When hydrogen is passed through a fuel cell, it chemically fuses with oxygen from the air. This reaction produces electricity, which powers the motor inside the vehicle.

Fritz Haber on a German postage stamp

Hindenburg disaster

In 1936, the German airship *Hindenburg* was the biggest aircraft ever built. It was filled with hydrogen, which easily catches fire and burns with an extremely hot flame. In 1937, the *Hindenburg* burned when the hydrogen gas began to leak and caught fire. The accident killed 36 people.

Making ammonia

The combination of hydrogen and nitrogen produces ammonia, which is used to make fertilizers that aid plant growth. Known as the Haber Process, this technique was developed by the German chemist Fritz Haber in the early 20th century and is still widely used.

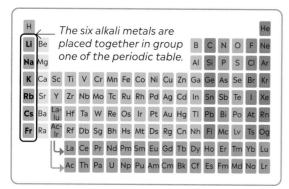

Alkali Metals

The first group of the periodic table is the alkali metals. A collection of six similar elements, these metals react vigorously with water to produce hydrogen gas and alkaline solutions, and with the oxygen in air to produce compounds called oxides. Alkali metals are highly reactive and are only found in nature combined with other elements in compounds. Pure alkali metals are shiny and soft enough to be cut with a knife.

Lithium

Li 3

Pure lithium is so light that it floats on water. However, if left in the open, this silvery metal will tarnish in minutes. To prevent this from happening, it has to be stored in mineral oil. Discovered in 1817, lithium has a wide range of commercial uses today. For instance, it is mixed with magnesium and aluminum to form lightweight alloys used to manufacture some aircraft and trains, and it's a key element in rechargeable batteries. Lithium is also useful in medications.

A dull oxide layer instantly forms on this pure alkali metal when it's exposed to air.

Laboratory-refined piece of pure lithium

In nature

An important source of lithium is lepidolite. This lilac-gray mineral gets its name from two Greek words: *lepidos*, which means "scales," and *lithos*, meaning "stone." It is so named because it forms flaky, scale-like crystals.

Soaking it up

Minerals containing lithium dissolve easily in water. The seas and ocean are filled with vast amounts of lithium. Sea creatures, such as the common lobster, absorb it from the water.

Powerful battery

Rechargeable lithium-ion batteries are widely used in modern electronic devices, such as smartphones. Not only are they lightweight and small; these batteries also allow people to use their cell phones for a long time between charges.

Sodium

11 Na One of the most widespread elements on Earth, sodium is highly reactive and is always found combined with other elements. It is essential for life, and sodium chloride (table salt) is the most common sodium compound. Sodium compounds are found in everything from baking powder to fireworks, and salt is also used to de-ice slippery roads.

Transparent, cube-shaped crystal

Halite

The mineral halite contains sodium chloride. More commonly known as rock salt, this compound is vital for human and animal health. Halite is found as cubic crystals and forms as deposits around seas and lakes in dry climates when the saltwater evaporates.

Dead bodies were dried using natron.

Preserved forever

Uses for sodium go all the way back to ancient Egypt. The Egyptians believed in an afterlife, and they preserved the dead in a process called mummification. They used a mineral called natron—a mixture of different sodium compounds—to absorb the water in the body to dry it out before wrapping it in linen.

Pure sodium in an airless vial

Baking powder

Sodium hydrocarbonate—better known as baking soda—is added to cake batter in baking. During cooking, the baking soda releases carbon dioxide gas, which helps the batter rise, giving the cake a light, airy texture.

Heap of sea salt in a salt farm

Harvesting salt

Salt forms in some rocks, and, over time, it dissolves and runs into seawater. In shallow pools, wind and the sun evaporate the water, leaving thick heaps of salt that can be collected by farmers.

Soft metal

Potassium is a soft metal that can be cut with a knife. This shiny, silvery metal tarnishes quickly when it reacts with oxygen in the air. This reaction forms a dull layer on the metal's surface. Cutting the metal again reveals the shiny surface once more.

Layer of a compound called potassium oxide

Potassium

19 K

With its low density, potassium is a typical group one metal. Like all alkali metals, potassium reacts with water to form an alkaline solution and flammable hydrogen gas. It is a key ingredient in many industrial products, such as fertilizers, plays a key role in regulating our muscular and nervous systems, and is important in our diet.

Potassium-rich foods

Banana

Celery

Coconut

Potassium in food

Several foods contain potassium. This useful element keeps the brain, nerves, and muscles functioning normally. Bananas are often considered to be potassium-rich, but many other foods have higher percentages of potassium. A cup of coconut water, for example, has 0.02 oz (600 mg) of potassium, compared to 0.015 oz (422 mg) in a banana.

Sylvite

A naturally occurring mineral of potassium, sylvite is composed mainly of the compound potassium chloride. Sylvite is similar to halite, which is also known as sodium chloride or simply "salt."

Pink match head contains sulfur and potassium chlorate.

Explosive quality

Potassium chlorate, a compound of potassium, chlorine, and oxygen, is used in the manufacture of matches. When a match is struck, phosphorus and potassium chlorate mix in small amounts and then ignite.

Plant food

Potassium is an essential element for plant growth. Its compounds are used extensively in fertilizers, along with phosphorus and nitrogen. In fact, fertilizers are often referred to by their "NPK" (nitrogen, phosphorus, potassium) content.

Potassium-based fertilizer sprayed on a field

Rubidium

37 Rb

From *rubidius*, which is Latin for "deep red," rubidium produces a red-colored flame when burned. Discovered by the German chemists Gustav Kirchhoff and Robert Bunsen in 1861, it has a low melting point of 102.2°F (39°C).

Pure rubidium is contained in this glass to prevent it from coming into contact with air and undergoing a violent reaction.

Laboratory sample of pure rubidium in an airless vial

Fireworks

When heated in a hot flame, compounds containing group one elements produce vivid colors. Rubidium produces a red-violet flame, and rubidium nitrate is sometimes used in fireworks to give this color. It is also an ingredient in illumination flares used by the military to aid rescues and at sea as distress signals.

Cesium

55 Cs

One of the most important applications of cesium is in making atomic clocks—accurate timekeeping devices that can measure time down to a nanosecond (one thousand-millionth of a second).

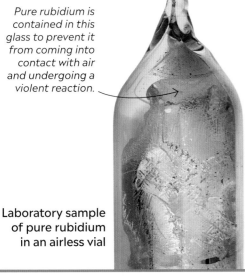

Pure cesium has a silvery-gold color.

Laboratory sample of pure cesium in an airless vial

Solar cells

Adding cesium to a solar cell boosts the conductivity of silicon in the glass, increasing the cell's efficiency. Solar cells have a wide range of applications, such as powering satellites in space.

Cesium-coated solar cell

Francium

87 Fr

This is one of the rarest elements on Earth, with only a few grams estimated to exist in the planet's crust. This scarcity meant that francium was one of the last elements to be discovered, in 1939, by the scientist Marguerite Perey. It was named after her native country—France.

Uraninite

This mineral contains tiny amounts of francium, a result of the atoms of other elements in the ore undergoing radioactive decay.

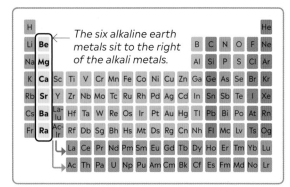

The six alkaline earth metals sit to the right of the alkali metals.

Alkaline Earth Metals

A slightly less reactive bunch than their group one neighbors, the group two elements are called "alkaline" because they form alkaline solutions when reacting with water. Soft and shiny when pure, they are called "earth metals" because many of them were discovered in their raw form in Earth's crust. First purified in the 19th century, all alkaline earth metals are solid at room temperature. Each element in this group burns with a distinctive color.

Beryllium

4 Be This element is named after the mineral beryl. Beryllium is released from the burning of fossil fuels and tobacco. This makes it a health hazard because it is chemically similar to magnesium and replaces it in the body, causing damage to cells. However, it has many applications when alloyed with other elements, such as in making missiles and satellites.

Aquamarine raw crystal

Aquamarine

One chief source of beryllium is beryl, a naturally occurring mineral made up of beryllium, aluminum, silicon, and oxygen. Beryl can take on many different colors, depending on the impurities present. Aquamarine is a type of blue beryl gemstone: the presence of iron makes it blue.

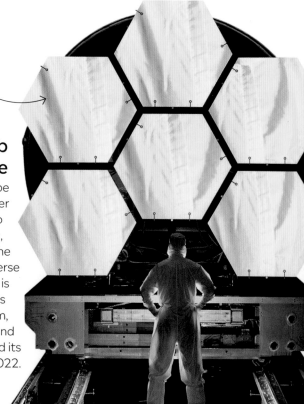

A single hexagonal mirror measures about 4.2 ft (1.3 m) in diameter.

James Webb Space Telescope

NASA's James Webb Space Telescope (JWST) was launched in December 2021. It has been designed to collect data about our solar system, planets around other stars, and the Big Bang with which our universe began. Light from distant stars is collected by an array of mirrors made of gold-plated beryllium, which makes the mirrors strong and lightweight. The JWST collected its first images in February 2022.

Magnesium

12 Mg

This lightweight metal is very reactive, including with oxygen in the air. When it burns, it produces a bright, white glow that is so intense, it can damage the eyes of anyone looking directly at the burning metal. Magnesium is used in flares and fireworks.

Yellowing leaves are a sign of magnesium deficiency.

Shiny, gray crystals

Laboratory sample of pure magnesium

Translucent crystals of magnesium carbonate

Brittle mineral

Magnesite

This mineral is mostly made up of magnesium carbonate, which is used in flooring, cosmetics, and even toothpaste. When heated strongly, it forms magnesium oxide, which is used to line furnaces due to its ability to resist heat.

Chlorophyll

Plants need sunlight to grow. Chlorophyll, a green-colored compound found in plants, absorbs light energy from the Sun, allowing plants to convert carbon dioxide and water into oxygen and sugars in a process called photosynthesis. At the center of each chlorophyll molecule is a magnesium atom.

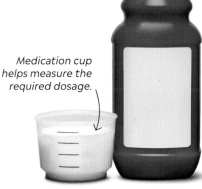

Medication cup helps measure the required dosage.

Tummy settler

Magnesium carbonate is added to medication used to ease heartburn and other stomach ailments. The carbonate reacts with excess acid in the stomach, producing water, magnesium chloride, and carbon dioxide gas in the process. The gas can make you burp!

Magnesium alloys

Alloys containing magnesium have the advantage of being both strong and lightweight. For that reason, several of them are used in the manufacture of high-performance machinery. One such alloy is called Mag-Thor: a mixture of magnesium, thorium, and other elements, it is used to build aircraft engines.

Finding magnesium

Magnesium and calcium were once thought to be the same element. In 1755, Scottish chemist Joseph Black (above) proved that they were different, but pure magnesium was only isolated in 1808 by Sir Humphry Davy.

These car rims are made of a magnesium-aluminum alloy for high strength and quality.

Custom-made car rims

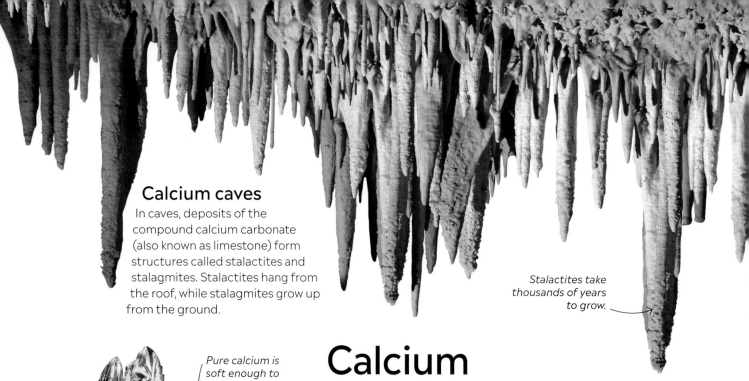

Calcium caves

In caves, deposits of the compound calcium carbonate (also known as limestone) form structures called stalactites and stalagmites. Stalactites hang from the roof, while stalagmites grow up from the ground.

Stalactites take thousands of years to grow.

Calcium

20 Ca

This soft metal is the fifth-most-abundant element in Earth's crust. As part of a mineral called hydroxylapatite, it strengthens our bones and teeth. Calcium compounds are also useful in industry and construction. For example, calcium oxide is used in the production of cement, while calcium hydroxide is used for treating sewage.

Pure calcium is soft enough to cut with a knife.

Crystals of pure calcium refined in a laboratory

Acid controller

Calcium compounds are used to reduce acidity in various ways. They are added to tablets that reduce acid-related discomfort in the stomach. Calcium supplements can also boost the growth of some plants by making the soil less acidic.

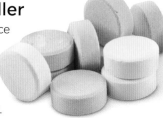

Indigestion tablets

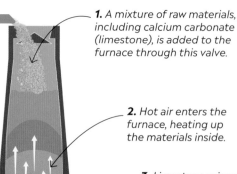

Teeth and bones

Calcium is the most abundant metal in our body. Calcium isn't only needed for strong teeth and bones—it also helps our cells work properly. We get calcium in our diet by eating calcium-rich food, including dairy products and nuts.

PRODUCING IRON

Calcium carbonate (limestone) is important in the production of pure iron. It is added to the raw materials in a blast furnace, where it removes sand and other impurities from the iron ore.

1. A mixture of raw materials, including calcium carbonate (limestone), is added to the furnace through this valve.

2. Hot air enters the furnace, heating up the materials inside.

3. Limestone mixes with the impurities in the ore to form a mixture called slag. This slag floats above the molten iron and is collected from the furnace.

4. Pure molten iron sinks to the bottom and is then drained from the furnace.

Strontium

38 Sr
This element is named after Strontian, a Scottish village near where its ore strontianite was discovered. Strontium has a toxic, radioactive isotope called strontium-90. Nuclear accidents, such as the 1986 disaster in Chernobyl, Ukraine, have released a large amount of strontium-90 into the atmosphere.

Signal flare

Compounds of the group 2 elements are used to produce colored flames. Calcium compounds give an orange-red color, while barium compounds produce green. Strontium compounds provide the bright crimson found in fireworks and signal flares (as pictured).

Barium

56 Ba
Discovered in 1808 by the English scientist Humphry Davy, the name of this highly reactive metal comes from the Greek word *barys*, meaning "heavy." Interestingly, it is not barium itself that is heavy but the minerals (such as baryte) in which it is found.

Barium meal

In this medical test, a patient swallows a "meal" of barium sulfate, a harmless compound that passes through the digestive tract. This allows a patient's digestive organs—highlighted by the barium compound—to be examined clearly using an X-ray photograph.

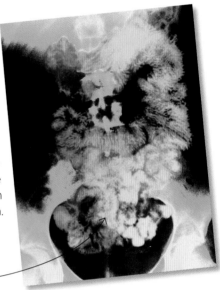

X-ray of a healthy human digestive tract, highlighted using a "barium meal."

Radium

88 Ra
A very radioactive element, radium gets its name from the Latin word *radius*, meaning "ray" (radium glows in the dark). In the early 20th century, radium compounds were used in medications because people believed that radium cured diseases. However, its use was phased out when people who took these drugs became unwell.

Glow in the dark

An isotope of radium, radium-226 was used in luminous paints to make watch and clock dials glow in the dark. The paints became popular in the 1920s, long before their health risk was fully understood. Many people, especially women, who worked with this paint became sick and even died as a result of exposure to radium.

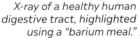

The radium in this paint makes the numbers glow green-blue in the dark.

This ore contains 0.02 oz (0.7 g) of radium in every 2,205 lb (1,000 kg) of rock.

Uraninite

Formerly known as pitchblende, uraninite is mostly uranium oxide as well as other elements that form as the uranium decays. Polish-born French scientist Marie Curie discovered both radium and polonium by processing huge amounts of uraninite. Polonium was named after Poland.

Marie Curie

In 1898, Marie Curie discovered radium and polonium, sharing credit for the former with her husband, Pierre Curie. She received the Nobel Prize in Chemistry in 1911 for these discoveries, becoming the first woman to win a Nobel Prize, and she remains the only woman to have received two.

Medal commemorating the 100th anniversary of Marie Curie's birth, 1967

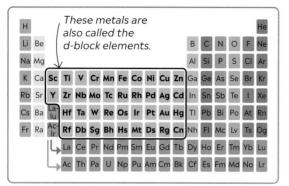

Laboratory sample of pure titanium

Transition **Metals**

With 38 members, the transition metals form the largest set of elements in the periodic table. They include those that sit in periods (rows) 4 to 6 and groups (columns) 3 to 12. Some characteristics do vary between members of this block of elements, but they are mostly similar. For example, all these metals are typically hard and shiny, have high melting and boiling points, and are good conductors of heat and electricity.

These metals are also called the d-block elements.

Titanium

22 Ti Named after the titans of Greek mythology—gods who were known for their exceptional strength—titanium is hard, strong, but also lightweight. It's a fitting name because most of the metal's applications are based on titanium having the highest strength-to-weight ratio of all metals, as well as its ability to resist corrosion.

Everyday use

Titanium is used to make items where strength is important, but the weight of the object must be kept low. Despite its higher cost, this metal has replaced steel and aluminum in some everyday items, such as eyeglass frames. Titanium is also useful in alloys—for example to make stronger steel.

Shine fades to gray when element is exposed to air

Lightweight titanium frame is durable and resistant to impact

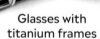

Glasses with titanium frames

Artificial arm made of titanium and carbon fiber

Artificial parts

This strong and light element is used in the medical industry to repair and even replace damaged or lost bones, joints, and limbs. Titanium plates, screws, and rods can also hold bones together as they heal. Titanium's ability to resist corrosion is also very important in medical applications.

Scandium

Sc 21

Although it sits with the d-block elements, scandium isn't technically a transition element because of the way its electrons are arranged. However, it has properties similar to its neighbors. Small amounts are mixed with other metals to make strong alloys.

Scandium is shiny but tarnishes quickly in air.

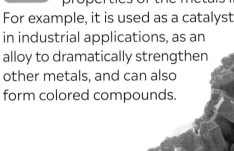

Laboratory sample of pure scandium

Dmitri Mendeleev predicted the existence of scandium ten years before it was discovered in 1879.

Lightweight strength

Scandium can dramatically strengthen aluminum, even when added in tiny amounts. One such application of the scandium-aluminum alloy is in the building of fighter jets, for which high strength and low weight are crucial.

Parts of this MiG-29 jet's fuselage are composed of a scandium–aluminum alloy.

Vanadium

V 23

A typical example of a transition metal, vanadium exhibits many of the common properties of the metals in this group. For example, it is used as a catalyst in industrial applications, as an alloy to dramatically strengthen other metals, and can also form colored compounds.

These brittle crystals are the main source of vanadium.

Vanadinite

Vanadium is extracted from an ore called vanadinite. The shiny red crystals are a naturally occurring compound made of vanadium, lead, oxygen, and chlorine.

Vanadinite

Chromium

Cr 24

Like vanadium, chromium can also form many colorful compounds—chromium is what gives the gemstone ruby its bright red color. The element was once an ingredient in pigments such as chrome yellow, but is no longer used because it is toxic.

Chrome finish

When plated on top of another metal, chromium gives machinery a polished, mirror look called the "chrome" finish. This was popular in the car industry in the 1950s and 1960s.

Chrome-plated body does not corrode easily

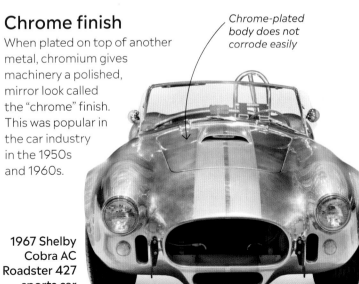

1967 Shelby Cobra AC Roadster 427 sports car

Manganese

25 Mn

The Swedish chemist Johan Gottlieb Gahn was the first to isolate pure manganese in 1774. This element is essential in our diet in small quantities. Cereals, nuts, beets, and various other fruits and vegetables, such as blueberries, avocados, and olives, are all good sources.

Cave art

Many pigments used in ancient paintings, such as the Lascaux cave paintings in France, come from compounds containing manganese. Oxides of manganese tend to produce brown and black colors.

Laboratory sample of pure manganese

This silvery metal is dense and brittle.

Better gasoline

A complex compound of manganese, carbon, hydrogen, and oxygen—known as MMT—is added to gasoline in some countries, particularly the US, to make cars run more efficiently. But as it is toxic, it's being phased out. Almost no MMT is used in fuel in the European Union today.

High-quality gas protects engines from wear.

Iron

26 Fe

Produced in huge quantities, iron is the most important metal used in the world today. While construction is its most common application, it is also used as a catalyst in many industrial processes, such as in the manufacture of ammonia for fertilizers. In human blood, iron is present in hemoglobin, a compound that carries oxygen around the body.

Iron power

When forged into weapons and machinery, iron brought economic and political power to many past empires. In the modern world, it is an important material in construction, often in the form of steel—an alloy of iron and carbon—but also as cast and wrought iron.

The Eiffel Tower, Paris, France

Wrought-iron lattice

Chunk of pure iron refined in a laboratory

Rust red

Iron corrodes in a natural chemical process called oxidation—rusting. When exposed to water and oxygen, its surface gets coated with a reddish-orange layer of hydrated iron oxide that cracks and flakes off, wearing away the metal.

Purple-pink crystals

Cobalt

27 Co

Cobalt is used to make permanent magnets (magnets that don't need electricity to work). Cobalt is important biologically—it is part of vitamin B12, which is important for making red blood cells. Alloys containing cobalt are hard-wearing and are used to make jet-engine blades and prosthetic body parts.

Coloring glass
In ancient times, a popular use of cobalt was in a pigment for coloring porcelain. In modern times, cobalt is often used to give glass a bright blue color.

Erythrite
A compound of cobalt, arsenic, oxygen, and water, erythrite is a mineral ore of cobalt. Bright red-purple in appearance, it is called "cobalt bloom" by miners.

Irradiating food
One particular form (isotope) of cobalt, cobalt-60, emits gamma radiation. This radiation can be used to sterilize surgical instruments and to preserve food by killing harmful germs.

This stained glass gets its blue color from cobalt.

Table lamp with blue glass lampshade

Nickel

28 Ni

This element's name comes from the German word *kupfernickel*, meaning "devil's copper." At first, German miners thought this mineral contained copper. It was later found to be an ore of nickel, but the shortened name—nickel—stuck. Pure nickel does not rust and is used to coat metal objects to protect them from corrosion.

Pure nickel balls refined in a laboratory

Tagging sea turtles
Nickel alloys are used to make numbered tags that help scientists track and identify individual marine creatures, such as sea turtles. Known as Monel tags, these are mixtures of nickel and copper and are highly resistant to corrosion in water.

These silvery-white pellets have a yellowish tinge.

Copper nickel
The 5-cent coin called the "nickel" is in fact three-quarters copper and only one-quarter nickel. Nickel appears in most "silver" coinage in the form of cupronickel, the alloy that nickel forms with copper.

The George Washington quarter, also made of cupronickel, was created in 1932 to commemorate the 200th anniversary of the president's birth.

Copper

29 Cu Found in minerals such as malachite, the color of pure copper makes it easily recognizable among metals. This element is very malleable and a good conductor of electricity. For this reason, it is useful in roofing, water pipes, coins, and electric motors.

Pellets of pure copper refined in a laboratory

Electrical wires

Copper is a natural choice for use in circuits and electrical wiring because of its ductility (the ability to be drawn out into thin wires) and its excellent electrical conductivity.

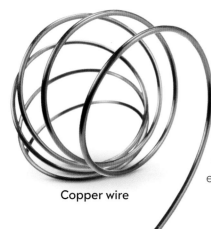

Copper wire

Making music

When mixed with zinc, copper forms an alloy called brass, which has long been used for making musical instruments. As copper is easy to shape, brass can be formed into complicated shapes to make these instruments—they also have a good acoustic quality and are very durable.

Brass saxophone

Green lady

Verdigris, a mixture of several copper compounds, is the green coating that forms on copper when it is exposed to air. The Statue of Liberty, in New York City, is now green because of verdigris on its copper layer.

Verdigris-coated copper layer sits on an iron framework.

Zinc

30 Zn A relatively common metal, zinc can be obtained from minerals such as sphalerite and smithsonite. This element is useful in many ways, mainly in compound form. Apart from being present in the alloy brass, its major use is in preventing the corrosion of steel. Its compound zinc oxide is commonly used as a white sunscreen cream.

Laboratory sample of pure zinc

In our diet

Zinc is essential in our diet. We consume it in foods such as cheese and sunflower seeds. Red meat—in the form of beef, liver, and lamb—is a particularly good source of zinc, as are herrings and oysters.

Sunflower seeds

This garden bucket's steel surface is galvanized to keep it safe from corrosion.

Galvanized bucket

Protecting steel

Steel can be shielded from corrosion by coating it with zinc—a process known as galvanization. The outer layer of zinc forms a barrier around the steel underneath, protecting it from exposure to air and water. Zinc is also a "sacrificial" metal, meaning it reacts in preference to the metal underneath it.

Yttrium

39 Y Along with three other elements—ytterbium, erbium, and terbium—yttrium is named after the town of Ytterby, in Sweden. Yttrium has a radioactive form, yttrium-90, which is used to treat some types of cancer.

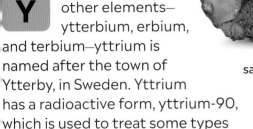

Laboratory sample of pure yttrium

YAG laser beam

Medical laser

When combined with other elements, yttrium can be used in laser surgery. A YAG (yttrium aluminium garnet) laser, when combined with an element called neodymium, is useful for cosmetic treatment, such as skin laser therapy.

Zirconium

Bar of pure zirconium refined in a laboratory

40 Zr This element gets its name from the Arabic word *zarkûn*, meaning "gold color." This is because its main mineral source, zircon, has a brownish-golden color. A shiny metal, zirconium is used to make hard-wearing alloys, such as those fitted in the outer layer of fuel rods in nuclear reactors.

Fake diamonds

Cubic zirconia, the crystalline form of zirconium dioxide, can mimic diamonds. These fake diamonds can also appear in various colors using other elements—for example, erbium makes pink cubic zirconia.

Molybdenum

42 Mo First isolated in 1781 by the Swedish chemist Peter Jacob Hjelm, molybdenum is an essential element in our diet. It is found in foods such as lentils and beans, and it helps clear some toxins in the body. One of its most important industrial uses is in the production of moly-steels—steel alloys with molybdenum added to them to make them harder and more resilient.

Element of war

Both the British and German armies used molybdenum during World War I. While the British used it to protect their tanks, the Germans used it for their heavy artillery.

British World War I Mark IV tank

Chunk of pure molybdenum refined in a laboratory

Steel-molybdenum body forms a protective layer against enemy fire

Niobium

41 Nb

Sourced mainly from the mineral columbite, the transition metal niobium has many uses: from pacemaker cases for the human heart to commemorative coins, jet engines, and rocket parts. Niobium-based magnets are used in MRI machines for medical imaging.

Rods of pure niobium refined in a laboratory

Artist's representation of the Apollo 15 Command/Service Module (CSM) spacecraft

Space exploration

Niobium is often mixed with other metals for specialist applications. It was used to make parts of the Command/Service Module spacecraft for the Apollo 15 mission to the moon.

This expansion nozzle was made of a niobium alloy.

Technetium

43 Tc

Originally thought not to occur in nature, it was later discovered that tiny amounts of technetium do exist as the result of the natural radioactive decay of uranium and thorium. It was not easy to find the element. Mendeleev predicted its existence as a missing element on his original periodic table. There followed many false claims of discovery, before Italian Carlo Perrier and Italian American Emilio Segrè finally isolated two of its isotopes in 1937. Its name comes from a Greek word meaning "artificial" because it was the first artificially produced element. Today, it is used mainly in medical imaging.

Ruthenium

44 Ru

This transition metal is mostly obtained as a by-product when other metals, such as nickel and copper, are purified. Ruthenium is often combined with platinum to harden electrical components. The element can also help speed up the industrial production of ammonia, a key ingredient in fertilizers.

Bright, silvery metal

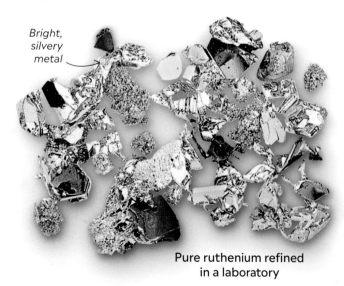

Pure ruthenium refined in a laboratory

Rhodium

45 Rh

This rare and hard metal is mainly obtained as a by-product during the refining of nickel and copper. One of rhodium's main applications is in making catalytic converters—devices that convert harmful exhaust gases into less dangerous ones—for cars. It is also used in many alloys to increase their resistance to corrosion.

Pure rhodium pellet refined in a laboratory

Rhodium-coated mirror makes the reflection of an object precise and sharp.

Special mirrors

Rhodium's ability to be polished to a bright shine means that it can be used in industrial and specialized mirrors, such as the mouth mirrors used by dentists.

Palladium

Pd 46

This precious metal is far rarer than silver or gold. It is used extensively in jewelry, particularly in "white gold," where gold is mixed with other silver-colored metals. A curious property of palladium is its ability to "soak up" hydrogen gas: at room temperature, it can absorb up to 900 times its own volume of hydrogen. Palladium is too expensive to use this way, but scientists have investigated the possibility of replicating this property in a cheaper material.

Pure palladium bar refined in a laboratory

Steel-gray mineral

Braggite

Although palladium is found pure in nature, it does also appear in some rare minerals, such as braggite. Discovered in 1932, this mineral also contains platinum, nickel, and sulfur.

Catalytic converter

Along with rhodium, palladium is used to coat the insides of catalytic converters for cars. Harmful gases, such as carbon monoxide, pass through the catalytic converter, where the palladium helps them react so they are converted into carbon dioxide, water, and nitrogen. These are then expelled by the car's exhaust systems.

Silver

Ag 47

This precious metal has been used for centuries, both as a form of currency and to craft jewelry. As the compound silver nitrate, it has been used as an antibiotic and a disinfectant. Some silver compounds, such as silver bromide, are light-sensitive; they change color when exposed to light. This property made the development of black-and-white photography possible.

Pellet of pure silver

Crystal-like structure

Chlorargyrite

One of the main ores of silver, chlorargyrite is chiefly composed of the compound silver chloride. It is colorless until it is exposed to light, when it turns brown and purple.

Using silver

Due to its shiny appearance, silver has been used in jewelry and in decorative items, from candlesticks to cutlery. One drawback of silver is that when exposed to air, it tarnishes easily to produce black-colored silver sulfide. As a result, decorative items that contain silver need to be cleaned regularly.

Cadmium

48 Cd This element was discovered in 1817 in a zinc-based mineral called calamine. In its pure form, the soft metal is silvery with a bluish tinge. Once a common ingredient in a variety of products, such as paint, cadmium is now known to be toxic and is used less and less.

This brittle mineral is easily chipped.

Ultraviolet (UV) light in this microscope is produced by a cadmium laser.

Pure cadmium pellet refined in a lab

Smithsonite
Named after the English chemist James Smithson, this mineral was first identified in 1802. Smithsonite mainly contains white zinc carbonate, but cadmium impurities give it a bright yellow color

High-intensity lasers
Powerful optical microscopes use cadmium lasers to study tiny specimens, such as microscopic organisms. The data collected by these lasers can then be pieced together to create 3-D images of the specimens, so scientists can study them further.

Hafnium

72 Hf Dmitri Mendeleev's prediction in 1869 about the existence of "element 72" encouraged Dutch physicist Dirk Coster and Hungarian radiologist Georg Karl von Hevesy to study zirconium ores. They discovered hafnium in 1923. Today, hafnium compounds are used to make specialized electronic circuits.

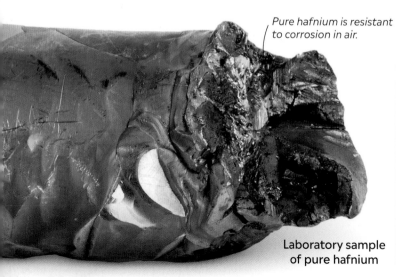

Pure hafnium is resistant to corrosion in air.

Laboratory sample of pure hafnium

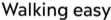

Rods of pure tantalum refined in a laboratory

Tantalum shell is flexible and lightweight.

Walking easy
Tantalum body implants are more porous than titanium, and tantalum bonds directly to bone, which encourages bone growth and keeps the implant firmly in place. Its ability to mimic the elasticity of bones has made tantalum an excellent choice for patients who need an artificial joint.

Artificial hip implant

Tantalum

73 Ta A hard metal that does not corrode easily, tantalum is combined with softer metals to make them stronger. Capacitors— devices used to store electric charge—in gadgets such as cell phones are often made of tantalum powder. It is also used to make artificial joints.

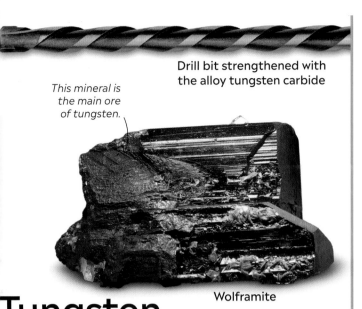

Drill bit strengthened with
the alloy tungsten carbide

*This mineral is
the main ore
of tungsten.*

Wolframite

Tungsten

74
W

Heavy and dense, tungsten has
the highest melting point of any
metal, turning to liquid at 6,177.2°F
(3,414°C). It was once used in light bulb
filaments, but these kinds of bulbs have now
been phased out because they are inefficient.

Osmium

Fountain pen

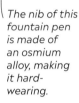

76
Os

The pure form of osmium forms
a poisonous strong-smelling
oxide when it reacts with
oxygen in the air. For safe use, it is
combined with other elements. From
fingerprint powder used in forensic
laboratories to nibs for fountain
pens, osmium alloys have many
specialized uses.

*The nib of this
fountain pen
is made of
an osmium
alloy, making
it hard-
wearing.*

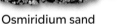

*This sand is
a natural alloy
of osmium
and iridium.*

Osmiridium sand

Rhenium

75
Re

Named after the Rhine
River in Germany, this
element was discovered
in 1925. Rhenium has the second-
highest melting point of all metals.
Its ability to withstand high heat has
made it very effective in superalloys
used in oven filaments, X-ray machines,
and jet aircraft turbine blades.

Pure rhenium
pellet refined in
a laboratory

Turbo engine

The Rolls-Royce Trent
XWB is a turbofan jet
engine used on the
Airbus A350 XWB
airplane. Its inner
blades, which are
made of a superalloy
that includes rhenium,
can withstand
extremely high
temperatures.

Iridium

77
Ir

In nature, iridium occurs as an impurity in
naturally occurring platinum. A thin layer
of iridium is also present in Earth's crust.
Some scientists believe that the meteorite that
triggered the death of the dinosaurs 66 million
years ago also distributed this layer of iridium
across Earth with its impact.

Powerful
telescope

NASA's Chandra X-ray
Observatory, an Earth-
orbiting telescope that
studies X-rays from distant
stars, has eight iridium-
coated glass mirrors. The
coating helps catch and bounce
the X-rays toward the telescope's
scientific instruments that study
the rays and gather data.

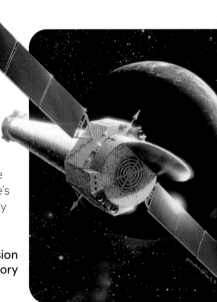

Artist's impression
of Chandra X-ray Observatory

This silver-colored metal can be polished to a bright silver-white finish.

Nugget of pure platinum refined in a laboratory

Platinum

78 Pt

This precious metal is quite rare, which makes it expensive. It is used in jewelry and also plays an important role in industry as a catalyst, such as in the production of nitric acid, which is used in making fertilizers.

Jewelry

As a beautiful, durable, and lustrous white metal, platinum has been used for making jewelry for centuries. It has a high resistance to corrosion, meaning that it stays shiny for a long time.

Platinum ring

Rutherfordium

104 Rf

An artificial element, rutherfordium is made by bombarding californium atoms with carbon atoms, and only a few atoms of it have ever been produced. It was first created in the 1960s, but due to controversy over the results, it wasn't formally named until 1996.

Naming rutherfordium

Element number 104 is named in honor of the New Zealand chemist Ernest Rutherford. He was one of the first scientists to conduct experiments that helped explain the structure of the atom. His "Gold Foil Experiment" determined that the atom had a dense nucleus.

Caricature of Ernest Rutherford

Mercury

80 Hg

People have been using this element for thousands of years. Around 10,000 years ago, the mercury-containing mineral cinnabar was used to make wall paintings in Çatalhöyük in modern-day Turkey. Pure mercury—sometimes called "quicksilver"—is the only metal that is liquid at room temperature.

Striking, deep-red mineral

Cinnabar

Cinnabar

As the main ore of mercury, cinnabar has been used for thousands of years. In 16th-century China, craftspeople painted wooden jewelry boxes with the bright red pigment extracted from cinnabar. This mineral was also once crushed into a powdered form for use as a cosmetic. Over the centuries, its use has declined due to mercury's toxicity.

Mercury thermometer

Polish-born Dutch physicist Daniel Gabriel Fahrenheit invented the mercury thermometer in 1714. His name is given to the Fahrenheit temperature scale that is still used in the US. In a mercury thermometer, the mercury expands and rises up the narrow tube as the temperature increases. Because of concerns over mercury's toxicity, these thermometers are being gradually replaced by safe, digital versions.

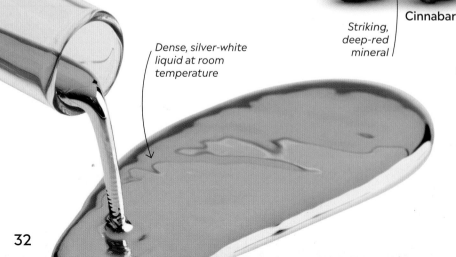

Dense, silver-white liquid at room temperature

Gold

79
Au

The chemical symbol for this element comes from the Latin word *aurum*, meaning "gold." This metal is found in its pure form and has been used in jewelry and decoration for more than 5,000 years. Alchemists—the forerunners of modern chemists—sought to convert relatively common metals such as lead into precious ones like gold.

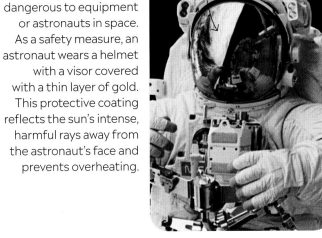

Flakes of pure gold refined in a laboratory

Gold in quartz

Gold is mostly found as veins in rocks such as quartz. These form when a hot mixture of minerals rises from deep within Earth in liquid form, then cools and solidifies near the surface. When these rocks are broken down, by weathering or river erosion, particles of gold are released.

Reflecting heat

The sun's heat can be dangerous to equipment or astronauts in space. As a safety measure, an astronaut wears a helmet with a visor covered with a thin layer of gold. This protective coating reflects the sun's intense, harmful rays away from the astronaut's face and prevents overheating.

Gold used as a reflective screen

Coins of gold

Pure gold and alloys that include gold have been used in coins since ancient times. Its shiny appearance, high value-to-weight ratio, and ability to resist corrosion made it a popular choice for use as money.

Coin issued by King Philip II of Macedonia (359–336 BCE)

Decorating with gold

Gold does not tarnish over time and as such has been used in buildings by architects since ancient times as an adornment. Gold leaf work and gold plating are common forms of decorations. The metal can even be used in flake and dust form to decorate food for consumption in some parts of the world, such as India.

The gold covering the Golden Temple in Amritsar, India, is not only decorative; it also resists corrosion.

Dubnium

Named after Dubna, the Russian town where it was first made, element number 105 is radioactive. Dubnium is an artificial element and currently has no uses beyond scientific research.

Controversial discovery

Two teams of scientists, one from Russia and the other from the US, claimed to have made dubnium at different times. The team in Russia was led by Georgy Flerov in 1968, and the US team was led by Albert Ghiorso in 1970. It wasn't until 1993 that the Russian team was credited with the discovery, and dubnium was officially named.

Albert Ghiorso (right) with James Harris, a fellow scientist

Seaborgium

Only a few atoms of this artificial element have ever been made. They were first created in 1974 at the Lawrence Berkeley National Laboratory, in California, by making californium atoms collide with oxygen atoms. Seaborgium is currently used only in scientific research.

Naming seaborgium

American chemist Glenn T. Seaborg worked with various teams during his career, creating many artificial elements. At the time, it was unusual to name an element after a living person, but he was honored in this way in 1993, before his death in 1999.

Cartoon of Seaborg

Bohrium

Used only in scientific research, this artifical element was discovered in 1981 by a team of German scientists firing chromium and manganese atoms at bismuth and lead. This element was named bohrium in 1997, despite worries that it might sound too similar to that of element 5, boron.

Niels Bohr

Bohrium was named in honour of Danish physicist Niels Bohr, who is best known for his work on the structure of the atom and his insight into atomic theory. His famous "Bohr model" of the atom earned him the Nobel Prize in Physics in 1922.

Niels Bohr in his laboratory

Hassium

This element was named after the German state of Hesse, which is home to the Centre for Heavy Ion Research—the institution where hassium was made in 1984. To create hassium, a team of scientists, led by the German physicist Peter Armbruster, crashed lead and iron atoms together. Like all of the super-heavy artificial elements, hassium's atoms are radioactive, meaning that they quickly decay to form other elements. Therefore, a pure sample has never been collected, but it's expected to be one of the densest elements.

Meitnerium

109 Mt

Named in honor of the Austrian physicist Lise Meitner, meitnerium was first created in Germany in 1982, when atoms of bismuth and iron were smashed into one another. This radioactive element has no known uses outside research.

Meitner and Hahn

The German chemist Otto Hahn singly won the Nobel Prize in Chemistry in 1944 for his and Meitner's work on nuclear fission. Meitner went on to have a new element named after her.

Otto Hahn (left) and Lise Meitner

Darmstadtium

110 Ds

First created in 1994 in the German city of Darmstadt, darmstadtium was later named after this city. Only a few atoms of this highly radioactive element have ever been made. Little is known about this element, but it's expected to be similar to palladium and platinum.

Sigurd Hofmann

A team led by the German physicist Sigurd Hofmann first created darmstadtium by smashing nickel and lead atoms into one another. Hofmann also worked on the creation of two other artificial elements—roentgenium and copernicium.

Roentgenium

111 Rg

As this element is placed directly below gold on the periodic table, some scientists believe it is likely to share some of gold's characteristics. It was first made in 1994 by smashing together nickel and bismuth atoms. It was informally known as E111 before being officially named roentgenium in 2004.

Wilhelm Röntgen

Roentgenium is named in honor of the German physicist Wilhelm Conrad Röntgen, the discoverer of X-rays.

Copernicium

112 Cn

A highly radioactive element, copernicium was first made in 1996 when atoms of zinc were made to collide with lead atoms. Some scientists think it is likely to be a gas at room temperature, but it might theoretically form bonds with other metals, such as copper and palladium.

Paying homage

Copernicium was named after the 16th-century Polish astronomer Nicolaus Copernicus, who formulated a model of the universe with the sun, rather than Earth, in the center. This is a statue of him in front of Olsztyn Castle, where he lived.

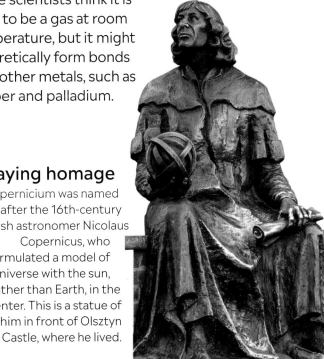

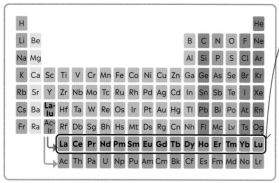

Lanthanides

Once known as the "rare earths," the lanthanides are, in fact, not rare at all, but they are similar to each other. This made them difficult to separate at first—the name "lanthanide" means "like lanthanum," and in Greek, *lanthano* means "hidden."

The lanthanide series—the collective name for elements 57-70—is named after lanthanum, the first element in this series.

Lanthanum

57 La

This lanthanide was discovered by the Swedish chemist Carl Gustaf Mosander in 1839. One of its compounds—lanthanum oxide—is added to the glass used in some camera and telescope lenses to give sharper images. Small amounts of lanthanum are added to some steels to improve impact resistance.

Bastnäsite
This mineral is a mixture of three metals: yttrium, cerium, and lanthanum, combined with carbon, oxygen, and fluorine. Bastnäsite is used as a source of each of those elements, which are extracted from the ore in a complex process.

Neodymium

60 Nd

In 1885, the Austrian chemist Carl Auer von Welsbach extracted this element from didymium, a mixture of neodymium and praseodymium. It's used to make powerful magnets and lasers, including some types of laser pointers.

This silvery-white metal will tarnish quickly in air.

Laboratory sample of pure neodymium

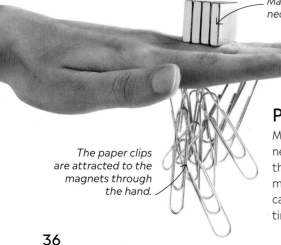

Magnets made from an alloy of neodymium, iron, and boron

The paper clips are attracted to the magnets through the hand.

Powerful magnets
Mixed with iron and boron, neodymium makes some of the strongest permanent magnets. Such magnets can lift items a thousand times their own weight!

Promethium

61 Pm

Promethium was first discovered in the fission products of uranium in 1945 and was named after Prometheus, the Titan in Greek mythology who stole fire from the gods. At the end of World War II, and with nuclear weapons in mind, this was intended to symbolize the possible dangers of scientific discoveries.

Promethium-rich paint

Paints
Mixed with zinc sulfide, promethium is added to paint to give a green-blue glow. The manufacture of "glow-in-the-dark" watch dials using promethium was once popular, but this application has been largely phased out.

Cerium

58
Ce

In 1803, cerium was discovered and named after the dwarf planet Ceres (which itself was named after the Roman goddess of agriculture) by one of its discoverers, Swedish chemist Jöns Jakob Berzelius. An important use of cerium is in white LEDs, and it's also used to make some fade-resistant pigments.

Laboratory sample
of pure cerium

Praseodymium

59
Pr

A part of praseodymium's name comes from the Greek word *prasios*, meaning "green," because it turns green when it tarnishes in air and forms other bright green compounds. Combined with neodymium, praseodymium is used to create high-power magnets.

Laboratory sample of
pure praseodymium

Filter for safety glasses

Praseodymium is used to give a colored tint to the safety glasses used by welders and glassblowers. The tinted goggles filter out the potentially damaging ultraviolet radiation, protecting the eyes of the wearer.

These glasses from the 1920s contain praseodymium that makes them green.

Samarium

62
Sm

This element was discovered by French chemist Paul-Émile Lecoq de Boisbaudran and named after the mineral samarskite from which it was first extracted. Samarium is added to cobalt to make powerful magnets that are useful because they continue to work at high temperatures.

Laboratory samples of
pure samarium

Europium

63
Eu

Paul-Émile Lecoq de Boisbaudran found europium first in 1892, but its discovery is usually credited to the French chemist Eugène-Anatole Demarçay, who isolated it in 1901. It's used in the inks used to print euro banknotes—under ultraviolet (UV) light, the notes glow red, proving they are genuine.

Laboratory sample of pure europium

Gadolinium

Gd 64

Named after the Finnish chemist Johan Gadolin, gadolinium can be used to treat tumors in a treatment called neutron therapy. Alloys made with small amounts of this element can resist high temperatures.

Laboratory sample of pure gadolinium

Soft, silvery metal

Gadolinium MRI scan of a healthy human brain and eyes

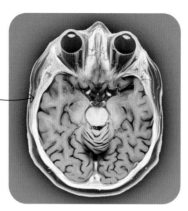

Gadolinite

This black mineral only contains very tiny amounts of gadolinium. Its composition varies but usually has cerium or yttrium mixed with other elements.

Clear images

A non-toxic form of gadolinium is used in MRI (magnetic resonance imaging) scans as a contrasting agent to help improve the quality of the images of internal body structures.

Terbium

Tb 65

Terbium was discovered by Swedish chemist Carl Mosander, who detected it as an impurity in yttrium oxide. It's one of four elements named after the tiny Swedish village of Ytterby—the others are erbium, yttrium, and ytterbium, and all were isolated from gadolinite, which was mined there. Because of their similarities, the elements were confused in the 19th century, and the names of erbium and terbium ended up switched. Today, terbium is used in fuel cells, in special alloys, and to make some types of fluorescent lamps.

Dysprosium

Dy 66

The Greek word *dysprositos*, for which dysprosium is named, means "hard to get." Like other lanthanides, this element occurs in nature combined with other members of its group and is hard to extract. Despite its discovery in 1886, dysprosium was not isolated until the 1950s. Today, it's mostly used in nuclear reactors and to make magnets.

Generating energy

Dysprosium's main commercial use today is as an alloy with neodymium, iron, and boron in making powerful magnets. Strong and lightweight, these magnets help run many wind turbines.

Wind turbines at Dun Law Windfarm, Scotland, UK

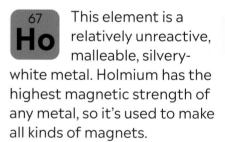

Holmium

Ho 67

This element is a relatively unreactive, malleable, silvery-white metal. Holmium has the highest magnetic strength of any metal, so it's used to make all kinds of magnets.

The red color in this zirconia gemstone comes from holmium oxide.

Rich color

Holmium impurities can give a red or yellow color to a zirconia gemstone. The compound holmium oxide can also be used to color glass.

Erbium

68 Er

This silvery metal is used in the form of its compound erbium oxide to add a pink color to glassware, ceramic glazes, and cubic zirconia gemstones. It's also used to make lens filters for photography and for certain types of laser.

Laboratory sample of pure erbium

These safety goggles contain erbium.

Protective goggles

Erbium oxide is added to glass used in protective goggles worn by welders and glassblowers. This glass absorbs the ultraviolet radiation that can damage our eyes.

Thulium

69 Tm

Not to be confused with the similarly named thallium, pure thulium was first isolated in 1911 by the Swedish chemist Per Teodor Cleve. It's found in X-ray machines used by doctors and dentists.

This metal is soft enough to cut with a knife.

Laboratory sample of pure thulium

Ytterbium

70 Yb

This soft metal reacts with air to form a layer of golden-brown oxide compound on its surface. A small amount of ytterbium is sometimes used to strengthen steel. Its compounds are also used in lasers.

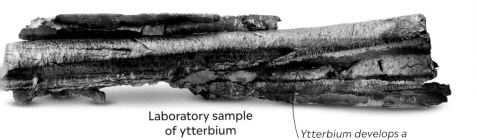

Laboratory sample of ytterbium

Ytterbium develops a golden color in air.

Standardizing time

Inside this highly sensitive optical clock, ytterbium atoms oscillate in response to the light of a laser beam. Counting these oscillations helps keep time accurately.

Optical clock, National Physical Laboratory, Teddington, UK

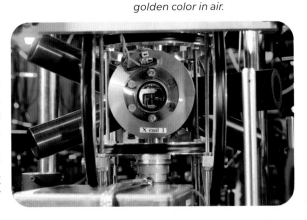

Lutetium

71 Lu

Like most other lanthanides, lutetium's principal ore is also monazite. This element is a hard, silver-colored metal with a high density. There's more lutetium than silver in Earth's crust, but lutetium is very difficult to separate from other elements, so it's not widely used. Small amounts are used by the petroleum industry, and one of its radioactive isotopes—lutetium-177—is used in cancer therapy.

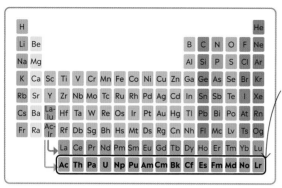

The elements with atomic numbers 89 to 103 are the actinides.

Thorium

90 Th A relatively common element, thorium appears in many naturally occurring minerals. Special glass with thorium dioxide was once used to make high-efficiency camera lenses, but the thorium made them radioactive. Research into using thorium as a nuclear fuel is ongoing.

Actinides

The elements in this series are fiercely radioactive metals. Most of them are either present only as decayed radioactive products or have to be artificially created. All the elements after uranium are called "transuranium" elements, and most of them are used mainly in research.

Brownish-red mineral

Monazite

The chief ore of thorium, monazite also contains varying amounts of the elements cerium, lanthanum, gadolinium, and neodymium. Depending on the exact composition, monazite varies in color from yellow to brownish-red.

Actinium

89 Ac A radioactive element present in Earth's crust in tiny amounts, actinium was first isolated in 1902. It gives the name to the actinide series. Because it is so scarce, there aren't many uses for it, but the isotope actinium-225 is being studied for use in some cancer treatments.

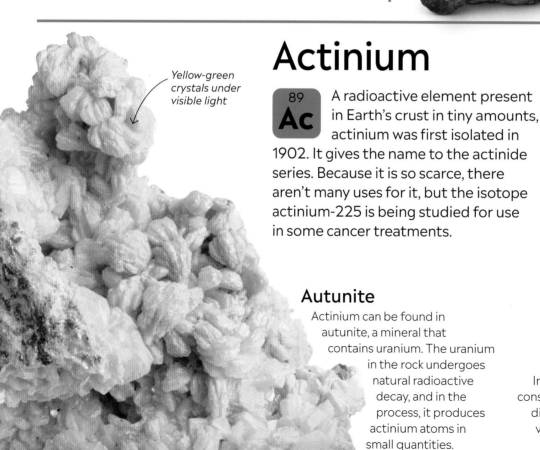

Yellow-green crystals under visible light

These vials for intravenous injections contain actinium, selenium, and radium.

Autunite

Actinium can be found in autunite, a mineral that contains uranium. The uranium in the rock undergoes natural radioactive decay, and in the process, it produces actinium atoms in small quantities. Autunite's crystals glow bright green under ultraviolet light.

Radioactive cures

In the early 20th century, radiation was considered by some as a cure-all for many diseases, and intravenous injections for various illnesses contained radioactive elements, including actinium. As radioactivity became better understood, it was discovered that these treatments had terrible health consequences.

Protactinium

91 Pa

The name protactinium comes from the Greek word *protos*—meaning "first"—coupled with actinium. It refers to the fact that protactinium is formed before actinium, in a radioactive decay sequence that starts with uranium. A form of protactinium is used by scientists to calculate the age of ocean sands.

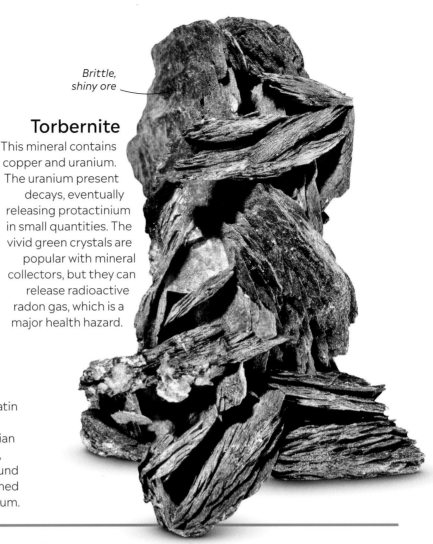

Brittle, shiny ore

Torbernite

This mineral contains copper and uranium. The uranium present decays, eventually releasing protactinium in small quantities. The vivid green crystals are popular with mineral collectors, but they can release radioactive radon gas, which is a major health hazard.

Lise Meitner

Protactinium was initially named brevium from the Latin word for "brief" because it was unstable. In 1918, Austrian physicist Lise Meitner (left), working with Otto Hahn, found a more stable form and named the new element protactinium.

Neptunium

93 Np

The discovery of neptunium in 1940 was an important one, as it was the first element after uranium to be artificially created. Its discovery opened up a new world of transuranium, or transuranic, elements. For their work in this area, the 1951 Nobel Prize in Chemistry was awarded to the US scientists Edwin McMillan and Glenn T. Seaborg.

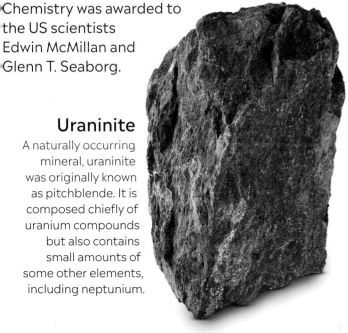

Uraninite

A naturally occurring mineral, uraninite was originally known as pitchblende. It is composed chiefly of uranium compounds but also contains small amounts of some other elements, including neptunium.

Americium

95 Am

Another artificially produced radioactive actinide, americium was first synthesized in the US in 1944. This element is only produced in nuclear reactors. It also emits rays that can be used to monitor the thickness of metal sheets in industry.

Detecting smoke

Americium's main commercial use is in detectors in smoke alarms. The safe radiation given off by americium allows an electrical current to flow, but if smoke enters the detector, its particles absorb the radiation, the circuit is broken, and an alarm sounds. Once the smoke clears, the current flows again, and the alarm turns off.

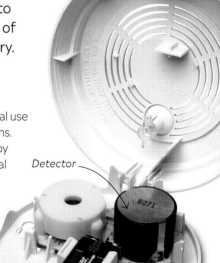

Detector

Uranium

92
U

This silvery-gray element changed the course of history. Its impact on the world, both in terms of its use as a nuclear fuel and in nuclear weapons, has been enormous. It was formally discovered by German chemist Martin Heinrich Klaproth, but arguably the discovery of radioactivity by the Nobel Prize–winning French physicist Henri Becquerel, through his study of uranium, opened the door to the nuclear age.

Chunk of
pure uranium

More than
8 million tons
of uranium can be found in Earth's crust.

Mining uranium

The Ranger uranium mine in the Northern Territory of Australia (right) is one of the world's largest sources of uranium. Once uranium ore is extracted from the ground, a series of chemical reactions are used to turn it into uranium dioxide. This is then used to make nuclear fuel rods for nuclear reactors.

This glaze contains up to 14 percent uranium.

Radioactive red

Fiestaware tableware was particularly popular in the 1930s. The red glazes that were applied to the plates, cups, and saucers included a significant amount of uranium oxide, which made them radioactive. The glaze was eventually discontinued, although non-radioactive Fiesta ceramics are still made.

Mushroom cloud

Since World War II, scientists have been able to harness uranium to create nuclear bombs. This process, called fission, occurs when a neutron strikes the nucleus of a particular form (isotope) of uranium atom and it splits, releasing a lot of energy and more neutrons. This starts a chain reaction, which becomes self-sustaining as the neutrons strike more nuclei. The resulting, often deadly, atomic explosion looks like a massive mushroom cloud.

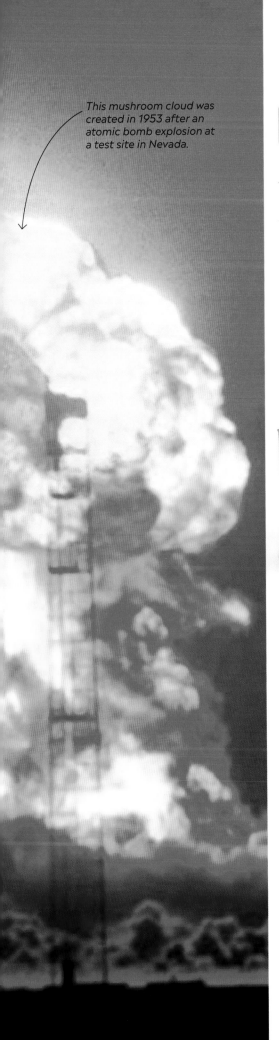

This mushroom cloud was created in 1953 after an atomic bomb explosion at a test site in Nevada.

Plutonium

94 Pu

Much like uranium, plutonium is used as a nuclear fuel—its most common application. Named after the dwarf planet Pluto, it was the first synthetic element that could be seen with the naked eye. It was discovered in 1940 in Berkeley, California, but its discovery was kept a secret until 1946 because the Americans were concerned about national security and plutonium's use in a nuclear weapon.

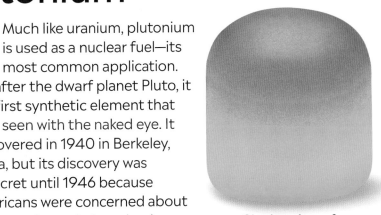

Glowing piece of plutonium oxide, the plutonium compound used as a nuclear fuel

Codename: Fat Man

Nuclear weapons were dropped by the US on Japan toward the end of World War II. The plutonium-based "Fat Man" atomic bomb was dropped on the city of Nagasaki in August 1945, just a few days after a uranium-based bomb was dropped on Hiroshima. The devastating nuclear fission reaction that took place in Nagasaki involved plutonium atoms splitting apart to release huge amounts of energy.

Replica of the "Fat Man" bomb, US Air Force Museum and National Aviation Hall

Artist's representation of the *New Horizons* spacecraft passing Pluto

Far from Earth

Launched in 2006 to study the dwarf planet Pluto, the *New Horizons* spacecraft carried about 22 lb (9.7 kg) of radioactive plutonium—enough fuel to keep its instruments running for 10 years. *New Horizons* made its closest approach to Pluto in July 2015.

Curium

96 Cm This radioactive element was named after the Polish-born chemist Marie Curie and her French husband, Pierre. Curium was discovered by American chemists Glenn T. Seaborg, Ralph A. James, and Albert Ghiorso in 1944. They produced the element in a cyclotron, a machine that smashes atoms into one another.

Marie Curie conducting an experiment in her laboratory

Californium

98 Cf Named after the state of California, californium was discovered in 1950 by the American scientists Stanley Thompson, Kenneth Street Jr., Albert Ghiorso, and Glenn T. Seaborg. This radioactive element is used in the treatment of cancer. It is also used in portable metal detectors.

Artificial creation

These pellets of californium were refined in a laboratory. The element is not found in nature and is created artificially by smashing atoms of berkelium with neutrons.

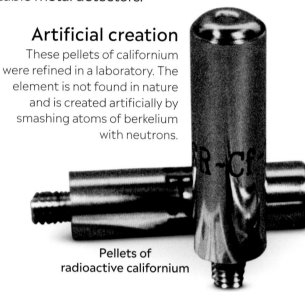

Pellets of radioactive californium

Berkelium

97 Bk This radioactive, silvery-white metal was named after the city of Berkeley in California, where it and several other elements were first made. In 1949, its discovery was led by a team of three American researchers—Glenn T. Seaborg, Stanley Thompson, and Albert Ghiorso. This element is so rare that it has no commercial or technological use today. In fact, only a little more than a gram of this soft element has been synthesized in the US since 1967.

Einsteinium

99 Es Discovered in 1952, this silvery, metallic element was named after the German-born physicist Albert Einstein. It was one of the two elements (along with fermium) to be identified while studying the remains of the "Ivy Mike" test—the first hydrogen bomb explosion.

Professor Albert Einstein

Fermium

100
Fm

The element fermium was named after the Italian physicist Enrico Fermi, the creator of the world's first nuclear reactor. Fermium is an artificial element useful only in scientific research.

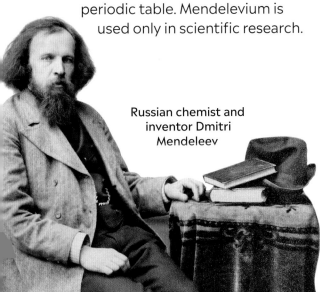

"Ivy Mike" test

The first successful test of a hydrogen bomb, in the Pacific in 1952, generated tiny amounts of fermium. This bomb was 1,000 times more powerful than nuclear bombs of the time.

Nobelium

102
No

American scientists Albert Ghiorso and John R. Walton and Norwegian physicist Torbjørn Sikkeland are credited for the discovery of this element. They created nobelium by making atoms of curium smash into carbon atoms in a cyclotron. It was named after the Swedish chemist and engineer Alfred Nobel. Nobelium has no uses outside of scientific research.

The Nobel Prize medal has Swedish inventor Alfred Nobel's face embossed on it.

Mendelevium

101
Md

In 1955, a new element was produced by smashing together atoms of einsteinium and helium in a cyclotron. By atomic number, it is the first element that cannot be produced in visible quantities. It was named after Dmitri Mendeleev, the creator of the modern periodic table. Mendelevium is used only in scientific research.

Russian chemist and inventor Dmitri Mendeleev

Lawrencium

103
Lr

Like many other artificially created elements, lawrencium is used only in scientific research. The American nuclear physicist Albert Ghiorso discovered lawrencium at the Lawrence Berkeley National Laboratory, in California, by firing boron atoms at californium atoms in a cyclotron. This element was named in honor of Ernest Lawrence, inventor of the cyclotron.

American physicist Ernest Lawrence with a cyclotron

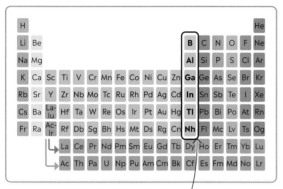

Group 13 of the periodic table houses the boron group.

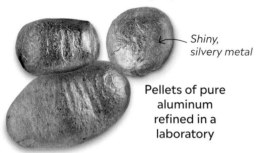

Shiny, silvery metal

Pellets of pure aluminum refined in a laboratory

The Boron **Group**

Except for the metalloid boron, all the elements in this group are metals. Aluminum is abundant in Earth's crust but takes a lot of energy to extract. Pure gallium is shiny and melts at just above room temperature. Indium forms compounds that are essential in many modern electronics, while thallium is a deadly poison. Scientists know very little about nihonium—the only artificial element in this group.

Aluminum

13 Al

This element is the most abundant metal in Earth's crust, in the form of aluminum oxides, and the third most abundant among all elements, after oxygen and silicon. A light and strong metal, aluminum has a huge number of applications in industry and construction, particularly in building aircraft.

👁 EYEWITNESS

IRÈNE JOLIOT-CURIE
By bombarding a thin piece of aluminum with the nuclei of helium atoms, Irène Joliot-Curie (the daughter of Marie Curie) was the first to show it was possible to produce an element artificially—in this case, a radioactive form (isotope) of phosphorus.

Greenish-blue surface is soft and scratches easily.

Variscite
Many aluminum ores occur naturally. Variscite is formed when water rich in phosphates—naturally occurring compounds of phosphorus—reacts with aluminum-rich rocks. A striking green-blue colored mineral, variscite is sometimes mistaken for another gemstone, turquoise.

Boron

Dark, slightly shiny metal

Laboratory sample of pure boron

5 B

In nature, boron is essential in small quantities for healthy plant growth. Some boron compounds are antiseptic and antifungal, used to treat minor wounds. This hard metalloid is used to make a type of heat-resistant glass called borosilicate. Boron is also added to fiberglass to strengthen it.

Ooey-gooey slime

Borax—a compound of boron, oxygen, and sodium—is a popular household cleaning chemical. It can also be used to make slime, or flubber—a rubbery play material that flows through fingers like a thick fluid but behaves like a solid when squeezed.

Bright color comes from food coloring additives.

Keeping food fresh

As a metal, aluminum is malleable, meaning that it can be fashioned into very thin foil-like sheets. This foil is used in the packaging of food and medications. With a thickness of just fractions of a millimeter, it provides a complete barrier to light, oxygen, moisture, and bacteria.

Heat-resistant foil

Recycling

Despite aluminum being the most widely available metal on Earth, extracting it is an expensive process. This is mainly due to the large amounts of electricity used to extract the metal from aluminum oxide, which has a high melting point. Recycling the metal—by making soft drink cans, for instance—is important for industry because reusing aluminum is 90 percent more energy-efficient than making new aluminum.

An average drink can contains about 70 percent recycled aluminum.

Transmitting electricity

Aluminum is an excellent conductor of electricity, and so it is an ideal metal for use in power cables. The light weight of the aluminum cables means that fewer pylons are required to support them, reducing the cost of construction and shortening the time it takes to build networks of cables.

Aluminum fuselage is lightweight, so the plane uses less fuel to fly.

Flying metal

Light, strong, and resistant to corrosion, aluminum is ideal for use in the manufacture of aircraft. A modern plane can contain up to 80 percent aluminum—used in its pure form as well as in many high-strength alloys.

Gallium

31 Ga Similar in appearance to aluminum, gallium is a soft, silvery metal. However, unlike aluminum, this element has a much lower melting point of 84.2°F (29°C)—a cube of pure gallium will melt in your hand due to body heat. Some compounds of gallium are useful in semiconductors and are common in the electronics industry.

Needle-like crystals

Solid piece of pure gallium melting

Diaspore

Minerals that contain gallium are rare, but very small amounts of it can be found in ores such as the aluminum oxide mineral diaspore. Trace amounts of gallium are present in some other ores, including sphalerite, germanite, and bauxite.

Diaspore

Rover Zoë is powered only by its solar panels.

Rover Zoë in the Atacama Desert

Searching for life

Zoë is a rover built at Carnegie Mellon University, in Pennsylvania. Its solar panels generate power using cells made of a compound called gallium arsenide. In 2005, this rover was used for the first time in South America's dry Atacama Desert to search for signs of microscopic life. It returned in 2013 with a long drill, to look beneath the desert's surface. The goal is to develop technologies to explore Mars.

Array of colors

Gallium arsenide is one of the gallium compounds that can convert electricity to light in LEDs (light-emitting diodes). Available in many colors, LEDs are up to 80 percent more energy-efficient than traditional light bulbs and have many uses—from lights in homes to traffic lights and vehicle lights.

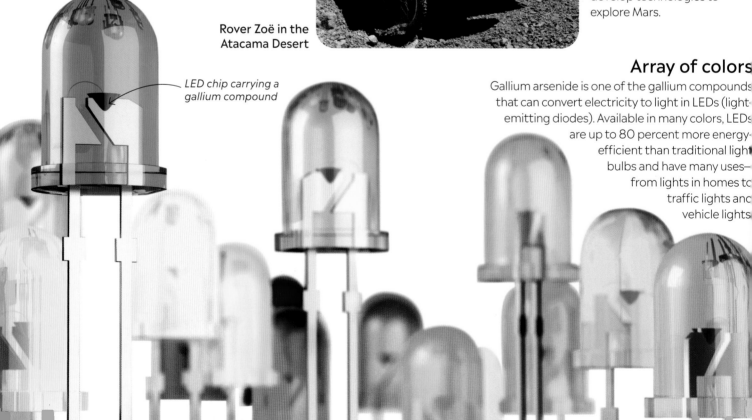

LED chip carrying a gallium compound

Indium

49 In

This element is named after the vivid indigo color that its atoms emit when electricity passes through it. Indium is generally found in nature combined with a mineral containing zinc or iron. Today, it is commonly used to make touchscreens. Like tin, it is also known as a metal that produces a shrieking noise when bent.

Pure indium mold cast in a laboratory

Indigo discovery

Indium salts, which are a type of indium compound, produce an indigo-blue color when heated strongly. German chemist Ferdinand Reich, the original discoverer of indium, was color-blind and needed his colleague Hieronymus Richter to see the indigo line in indium's color spectrum. When Richter claimed the element's discovery for himself, the two men fell out.

Extracting indium

Traces of indium can be found in several minerals, including sphalerite, quartz, and pyrite. However, the element is often collected as a by-product in the production of zinc and copper.

Sphalerite

Making touchscreens

Indium is mainly used to make indium tin oxide, a compound in touchscreens and solar panels. With such a huge demand for touchscreens in modern electronics, indium's scarcity is a concern.

Indigo-blue flame

Thallium

81 Tl

This toxic element's name comes from *thallos*, the Greek word for a "green shoot" or "twig"—thallium emits a vibrant green color when directly inserted into a flame. Thallium was often used as a rodent poison before many accidental deaths led to a ban on its use in the US in 1972.

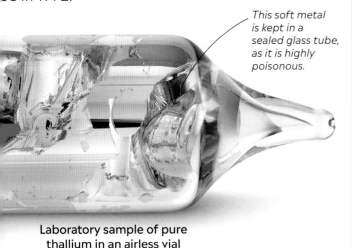

This soft metal is kept in a sealed glass tube, as it is highly poisonous.

Laboratory sample of pure thallium in an airless vial

Nihonium

113 Nh

Named and placed on the periodic table in 2016, nihonium is one of the most recent additions to the table. It is named after *Nihon*, the Japanese word for "Japan," the country where the element was created. It has no known uses.

History of discovery

Nihonium was first claimed by Russian research scientists, but ultimately a team from RIKEN (the Institute of Physical and Chemical Research) in Japan was credited with the discovery of element number 113.

Professor Kōsuke Morita, who led the team at RIKEN

The Carbon Group

The six elements of the carbon group sit between the boron group and the nitrogen group.

Like its neighbors on the periodic table, the carbon group is another mixed bag of elements. While carbon is a non-metal, silicon and germanium are metalloids. Tin and lead are metals that have been used in industry for millennia, while flerovium is an artificial element.

Carbon

6 C

Element number six is arguably one of the most important of all of the 118 known elements. All organic living things on Earth contain carbon atoms. Carbon atoms can form chemical bonds with each other to form large molecules and carbon produces millions of compounds, including those important for life—amino acids, fats, and DNA. From fossil fuels to diamonds, plastics, and all living organisms, carbon is everywhere.

Uncut diamond, a form of carbon

Colorless, crystalline mineral

Soft graphite

Glass-like carbon

This human-made material is called glassy carbon. It has a very high resistance to heat and does not easily react with oxygen. This means it can be used at high temperatures— for example, to make metalworking crucibles that hold molten metals.

Common carbon

Graphite and diamond are two especially common forms of carbon. Their distinctive atomic structures mean that they have very different properties: graphite is the soft and slippery material used in pencils, and diamonds are ultra hard precious gemstones also used as a cutting tool in industry.

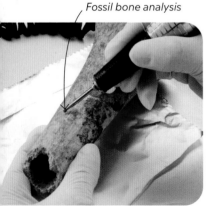

Fossil bone analysis

Carbon dating

A radioactive form (isotope) of carbon called carbon-14 is used to date ancient materials, such as bones. Over time, carbon-14 in an object breaks down, or "decays." The amount of carbon-14 in a sample is measured and compared with how long it takes for half of the radioactive carbon atoms to decay (the carbon's "half-life"). This gives scientists an estimate of the item's age.

Formula One race car

TOTAL

Silicon

14
Si

The second-most abundant element in Earth's crust, silicon forms most rocks. Its compound silicon dioxide is one of the major components of sand. Pure silicon is a bluish-gray solid. It's a semiconductor, which means it doesn't conduct electricity as well as a metal, but it's also not an insulator.

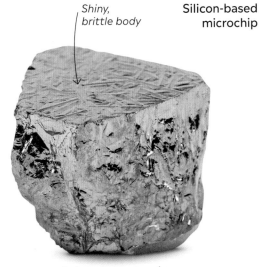

Shiny, brittle body

Laboratory sample of pure silicon

Silicon-based microchip

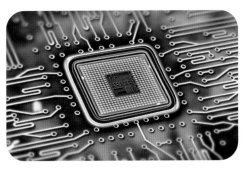

Microchips

Many modern machines work on microchips. A microchip stores and processes data and is made from a tiny wafer of silicon—a material that allows electrical signals to be transmitted precisely and quickly.

Plastic bag

Plastic box

Powerful plastic

Plastic is an artificial material made up of long chains of carbon atoms. Chemists can combine other elements—such as hydrogen, oxygen, fluorine, or chlorine—with carbon to manufacture different types of plastic for a variety of applications. Water resistant and relatively cheap, plastics have become very widely used. However, recently people have become worried about plastic pollution, and there have been moves to reduce the amount of single-use plastic we use.

Fossil fuels

Coal, natural gas, and oil are carbon-based fossil fuels—fuels formed in Earth's crust from the remains of ancient organisms. They form the basis of the world's energy supply, but concerns over pollution from burning them have led to the growing use of alternative energy sources.

Chimney releases pollutants.

Cooling tower releases water vapor

Light and sturdy

A lightweight, ultra-strong, human-made material called carbon fiber is used in the aerospace and car industries, where it can replace much heavier materials, such as steel. Race cars made of carbon fiber components are lighter and faster than earlier cars.

Tin

50 Sn

Mined since 3000 BCE, tin is combined with copper to form bronze, a strong alloy. Bronze played an important role in the development of many civilizations, allowing people to make weapons, tools, utensils, and statues. Tin is also combined with lead or other metals to make solder—a fusible alloy used to join metals together, especially in electronic devices.

Pale, silvery metal

Laboratory sample of pure tin

Auguste Rodin's bronze sculpture *The Thinker*, in Stockholm, Sweden

Bronze

Most modern bronze sculptures contain roughly 10 percent tin (the rest is copper). Harder, and more resistant to corrosion than iron, bronze has been an ideal material for sculptors for nearly 5,000 years. Modern applications also include propellers for ships and strings for guitars.

Tin toy train from 1900

Child's play

The malleability of tin made it useful in making toys over the last two centuries. Toys were often made with tinplate—a steel plate coated with a thin layer of tin. These days, such toys are collectible items—modern toys are more likely to be made of plastic.

Germanium

32 Ge

This brittle semi-metal was discovered in 1886 by the German chemist Clemens Alexander Winkler, and it is named after his home country, Germany. Germanium is an important element in technology, used in the production of high-quality lenses for microscopes and cameras.

Laboratory-refined germanium disc

Computer chips

Like silicon, germanium is a semiconductor, and it can be used to make microchips. It is combined to make silicon-germanium chips that work at high speeds, as shown here.

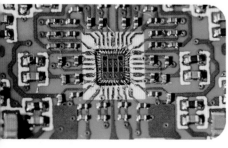

Flerovium

114 Fl

A synthetic element, flerovium was first produced in 1998 when scientists in Russia smashed together plutonium and calcium atoms. This highly radioactive element was given its official name in 2012. It sits in group 14, but scientists are still debating its properties. Some think it might have metallic properties, while others think it may behave more like a noble gas.

Georgy Flyorov

Flerovium is named after the Flerov Laboratory of Nuclear Reactions in Russia, where the element was discovered. The laboratory, in turn, is named after the Russian physicist Georgy Flyorov.

Lead

82
Pb

Like tin, lead and its compounds have been used for about 5,000 years. This gray metal is soft, malleable, and resistant to rust. In the past, it was used to make many things, including coins, plumbing pipes, and paint glazes. Awareness about lead's toxicity has limited its applications today, which still include car batteries, electricity cables, and decorative stained glass.

Dull gray metal

Pure lead refined in a laboratory

Shiny, green glaze

Brownish-yellow crystals containing a lead compound

Anglesite

This mineral contains a lead-sulfur compound that is one of the main sources of lead. Anglesite is produced in nature when oxygen reacts with galena—another ore of lead.

Chinese earthenware model of a pigsty from Later Han Dynasty, 206 BCE–220 CE

Lead glaze

The green glaze on this model of a pigsty from ancient China is made of lead compounds. When such a coating is applied to pottery, it makes it waterproof. Once fired in a kiln, the lead glaze becomes shiny.

Extra sparkle

Lead crystal—a type of decorative glassware—is glass that contains at least 24 percent lead oxide, which makes it heavier. It also bends light more than regular crystal and sparkles more as a result. Lead was used extensively in glassware before potential health risks over its use limited the manufacture of lead crystal.

Modern lead-acid car batteries are sealed and require no maintenance.

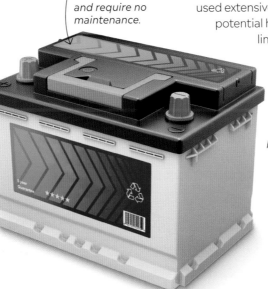

Lead power

The rechargeable batteries in gasoline and diesel cars are known as lead-acid batteries. This is because they contain lead plates, one of which is coated with lead oxide, in a solution of sulfuric acid. More modern electric vehicles are powered by lithium-ion batteries, but they sometimes have a lead-acid battery as well.

Lead crystal has a distinctive gray shade and a bright finish.

The Nitrogen Group

The six group 15 elements sit between the carbon and oxygen groups on the periodic table.

The metals, semi-metals, and non-metals in this group are known as the "pnictogens," from an ancient Greek word that means "to choke." This refers to the fact that someone breathing pure nitrogen would die from lack of oxygen—the name isn't really relevant to the other members of the group, as none of them are gases at room temperature.

Nitrogen

N 7

This element makes up 78 percent of Earth's atmosphere. An invisible and odorless gas, nitrogen is continually transferred between the environment and living things in a cycle. In the soil, nitrogen plays a vital role in the growth of plants and fungi. Animals make use of nitrogen to build proteins, which are essential to life.

Seen here stored in a glass sphere, nitrogen gas gives off a purple glow when electrified.

Nitratine

A compound of sodium, oxygen, and nitrogen, nitratine is one of the few naturally occurring minerals that are rich in nitrogen. It is found in dry, arid areas, and is usually white or pale pink in color.

The nitrogen cycle

Nitrogen is an essential element for Earth's ecosystem. It is recycled between the atmosphere, the surface, and living things—plants, animals, fungi, and bacteria.

1. Lightning causes nitrogen in the air to react with oxygen to form compounds, which mix with rainwater and then fall to the ground.

6. Bacteria in the soil break apart the nitrogen compounds, returning nitrogen into the air.

4. Animals take in the nitrogen compounds when they eat plant matter and release it in their dung.

5. Fungi break down the dung, which releases these compounds back into the soil.

3. The nitrogen compounds are taken up by plants.

2. Bacteria in the soil and plant roots also produce nitrogen compounds from nitrogen in the air.

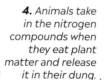

Phosphorus

15
P

Phosphorus is the most reactive member of group 15—white phosphorus ignites spontaneously in air. Phosphorus also plays a vital role in human biology. Like calcium, phosphorus strengthens bones and teeth. It is also present in deoxyribonucleic acid (DNA)—the chemical in our cells that carries our genetic information.

Apatite

This phosphorus-rich ore gets its name from the Greek word *apate*, which means "deceit," because apatite often resembles crystals of other minerals, such as aquamarine.

Taste matters

A 12 oz (350 ml) can of cola contains about 0.002 oz (60 mg) of phosphorus, in the safe form of phosphoric acid. This ingredient is widely used in soft drinks to bring out a tangy, sharp taste. It also prevents the growth of bacteria in the drink.

Glass of cola

It's a trap!

All plants need nitrogen in large quantities to grow. The Venus flytrap grows in nitrogen-poor soil, so it supplements its nitrogen needs by feeding on insects and absorbing the element from them. When insects land on its pressure-sensitive leaves, they close to form a stomachlike space. This trap then fills with liquid chemicals that dissolve the prey, which is slowly absorbed through the surface of the leaves.

Venus flytrap

Flies supply 75 percent of the nitrogen that this plant needs to survive.

Titan's nitrogen-rich atmosphere gets its orange-brown color from hydrocarbon particles.

Nitrogen-rich atmosphere

Saturn's largest moon, Titan, is unusual because it's thought to be the only moon in the Solar System with a substantial atmosphere. Its atmosphere is about 95 percent nitrogen, and the rest is mostly methane. Most scientists think that nitrogen may have been delivered to Titan's atmosphere by ancient comets that crashed into it.

Nitrogen-based fuel is twice as powerful as gasoline.

Fueling the race

Nitromethane is an immensely powerful fuel made up of carbon, hydrogen, and nitrogen. This fuel generates the force that accelerates dragsters to speeds of more than 300 mph (480 kph).

Arsenic

33 As One of the few elements that exhibit the properties of both metals and non-metals, arsenic is a metalloid. It is found in many minerals in Earth's crust, often combined with oxygen, chlorine, or sulfur. Arsenic rightly has a reputation as a deadly poison. However, some arsenic compounds have genuine medicinal uses, for example arsenic trioxide is used to treat a certain kind of blood cancer.

Volcanic vapor releases arsenic into the atmosphere.

Cluster of realgar crystals

Realgar

This arsenic sulfide mineral is found in hot volcanic springs and is an important source of arsenic. Realgar is toxic and has been used as a rat poison and a weedkiller.

DETECTING ARSENIC

In the early 1800s, arsenic compounds, which are tasteless and odorless, were sometimes used to poison food or drink without being detected. In 1836, the English chemist James Marsh devised a method (shown here) of detecting even the tiniest amounts of arsenic in food. This was called the Marsh Test.

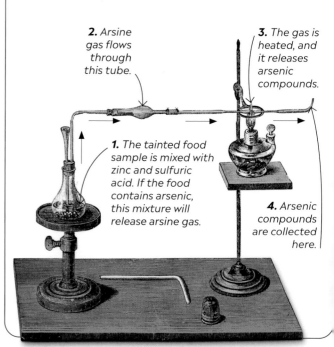

2. Arsine gas flows through this tube.

3. The gas is heated, and it releases arsenic compounds.

1. The tainted food sample is mixed with zinc and sulfuric acid. If the food contains arsenic, this mixture will release arsine gas.

4. Arsenic compounds are collected here.

Explosive gases

Many minerals in Earth's crust have high concentrations of arsenic compounds, and volcanic gases push these out into the atmosphere. When a volcano erupts, it releases a complicated mixture of chemicals at the surface, including a lot of arsenic. This can contaminate the air or nearby groundwater sources.

Antimony

Sb
51

This metalloid has two forms—one is a brittle, silvery metal, and the other is a non-metallic gray powder. Antimony's symbol—Sb—is not associated with its own name but comes from *stibium*, the Latin name for an antimony compound called antimony sulfide.

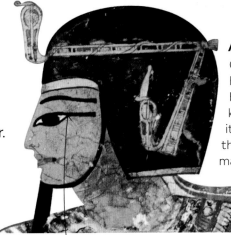

Ancient eye cosmetics

Compounds containing antimony have been used as black eyeliners by many civilizations. Known as kohl in some parts of the world, its use is controversial because the antimony and lead used to make it are toxic.

Painting of Egyptian Pharaoh Amenhotep I

Kohl is a dark eyeliner.

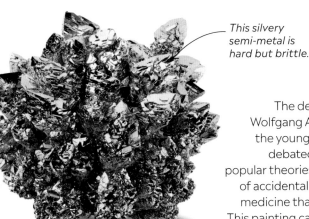

This silvery semi-metal is hard but brittle.

Pure antimony crystals refined in a laboratory

A sad note

The death of Austrian composer Wolfgang Amadeus Mozart in 1791 at the young age of 35 has been much debated by historians. One of the popular theories is that he died as a result of accidental antimony poisoning from medicine that he had been prescribed. This painting called *The Death Of Mozart* by Irish artist Henry O'Neill depicts the gifted composer's last moments.

Bismuth

Bi
83

A heavy metal with a low melting point, bismuth forms incredible rainbow-colored crystals. An oxide layer on the surface produces bright yellows, pinks, reds, and blues. As a result, bismuth was widely used to decorate items such as wooden chests. Bismuth has been used since ancient times, but for a long time it was confused with lead and tin—until it was proven to be a separate element in 1753.

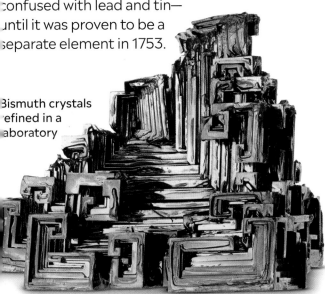

Bismuth crystals refined in a laboratory

Make-up

The shiny, "pearling" effect seen in cosmetics, such as nail polish, sometimes comes from a compound called bismuth oxychloride. When hit by light, its crystals produce a pearly sheen.

Moscovium

Mc
115

One of the newest elements to be placed on the periodic table, moscovium is named after Moscow, the capital city of Russia, where a significant amount of research for its creation was carried out. Moscovium is highly radioactive, and its atoms break up so quickly that it is hard to determine the element's properties, although some scientists think it may be a solid metal. Currently, it has no known applications.

The Oxygen Group

These elements are sometimes called "chalcogens," a combination of the Greek words *khalkós*, meaning "copper" and *genēs*, meaning "born" because they are often found in copper ores. Oxygen, sulfur, and selenium are non-metals, tellurium is a metalloid, and polonium is a metal. Only a few atoms of livermorium have ever been made.

The elements in group 16 are also known as "the oxygen family."

This glass sphere stores pure oxygen, which produces a silver-blue glow when electrified.

Oxygen

8 O

The third-most-abundant element in the universe, oxygen makes up 21 percent of the air we breathe. This colorless gas becomes a blue liquid at –297°F (–183°C), which is used in the medical industry to preserve tissue samples. Oxygen has several forms, including ozone, which forms a protective barrier between Earth and the damaging ultraviolet rays of the sun.

Oxygen reaction

A chemical reaction called oxidation occurs when oxygen comes into contact with any substance. For example, a cut apple turns brown because chemicals in its cells react with oxygen in the air. Rusting is a type of oxidation where iron reacts with oxygen and water to form flaky hydrated iron oxides that weaken the metal.

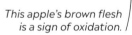

This apple's brown flesh is a sign of oxidation.

Oxygen cycle

Oxygen is essential for life, because all living things respire—use oxygen to release chemical energy from fuels such as sugars. However, while animals breathe in oxygen and breathe out carbon dioxide, plants take in carbon dioxide and, using sunlight and water, produce oxygen in a process called photosynthesis. They use some of this oxygen, but most is released back into the atmosphere, creating a cycle.

Specialized masks connected to oxygen tanks provide oxygen to the mountaineer.

Thin air

At high altitudes, such as on top of mountains, the air is thinner than it is at sea level. This means that the oxygen gas present is more spread out, which makes it difficult to breathe. Mountaineers, therefore, often carry a supply of oxygen in tanks.

Wood needs oxygen to burn, releasing heat and light.

Burning up

When something burns, it is said to be undergoing a reaction called combustion. This process involves three things: oxygen, a fuel (such as wood), and the release of heat (such as fire). If the supply of oxygen is removed, the fire will be extinguished.

 EYEWITNESS

Joseph Priestley

British chemist Joseph Priestley is usually credited with the discovery of oxygen, because he was the first to formally publish his results in 1775. But German-Swedish chemist Carl Wilhelm Scheele also has a claim to this element's discovery as he identified the gas and wrote about it in 1771.

Colorful sky

The northern lights—a naturally occurring display of light in some arctic regions—are the result of particles from the sun colliding with gases in Earth's atmosphere. Oxygen and nitrogen in the air are the gases responsible for the dazzling colors. The green color is produced when the sun's particles collide with oxygen, while the blue and violet colors are produced by their collision with nitrogen.

Selenium

34 Se

This non-metal has two pure forms—one is powdery and red, and the other is a hard, gray metal. Selenium is used to modify glass and to coat solar cells. Its compounds are found in many everyday products, from dandruff shampoos to photocopiers.

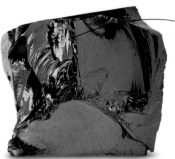

Metallic sheen on gray selenium

Chunk of pure gray selenium refined in a laboratory

Red color due to a selenium glaze

A touch of color

Certain selenium compounds can change the color of glass, such as providing an orange-red tint. Bright ruby reds or pink hues in glass are often due to the addition of selenium.

Tellurium

52 Te

Rare in Earth's crust, tellurium is named after *tellus*, the Latin name for "Earth." It's a toxic, silvery-white metalloid that is used in industry to make glass optical fibers and electronics.

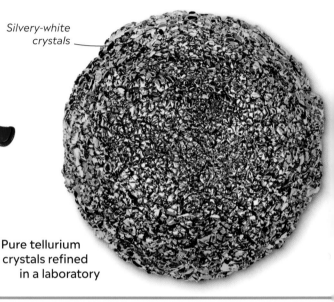

Silvery-white crystals

Pure tellurium crystals refined in a laboratory

Sulfur

16 S

Once believed to be an important ingredient in the making of the Philosopher's Stone—a legendary substance capable of turning common metals into gold—sulfur was used widely by early alchemists. In its raw form, this non-metal is found as yellow crystals. Pure sulfur has no smell, but its compounds often have egg-like smells. Sulfur is important for life—needed for healthy hair, skin, and muscles—and has lots of industrial uses, such as production of sulfuric acid.

Laboratory sample of pure sulfur granules

Celestine

Sometimes found in its pure native form, sulfur also appears in many compounds. The sulfur compound strontium sulfate is present in celestine, a pale blue crystalline mineral.

Sulfur springs

Volcanic hot springs are often a natural source of sulfur. The hot water in the springs is produced as a result of volcanic activity underground, and, as the water reaches the surface, it brings dissolved sulfur minerals with it. At this hot spring near the Dallol Volcano in Ethiopia, water containing sulfur has dried up, leaving behind a yellow crust.

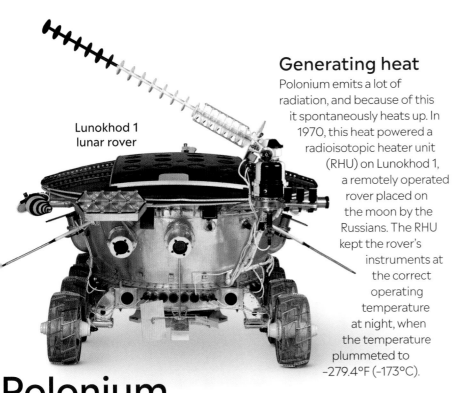

Lunokhod 1
lunar rover

Generating heat

Polonium emits a lot of radiation, and because of this it spontaneously heats up. In 1970, this heat powered a radioisotopic heater unit (RHU) on Lunokhod 1, a remotely operated rover placed on the moon by the Russians. The RHU kept the rover's instruments at the correct operating temperature at night, when the temperature plummeted to –279.4°F (–173°C).

Livermorium

116
Lv

Named in 2012, livermorium is an artificial, super-heavy element that was made by colliding curium and calcium atoms in a machine called a particle accelerator. It was discovered in partnership by Russian scientists at the Joint Institute for Nuclear Research (JINR) in Dubna, Russia, and American scientists at the Lawrence Livermore National Laboratory in California. Livermorium is named after this American laboratory. Little is known about this element, but scientists think it's likely to have similar properties to polonium.

Polonium

84
Po

This element was named after Poland, the birth country of its discoverer—Marie Curie. This silvery-gray metal is rare and highly radioactive, making it very dangerous to humans.

Vulcanization

Adding sulfur to rubber hardens the rubber and makes it flexible and more durable. This process is called vulcanization. Vulcanized rubber is up to 10 times stronger than natural rubber. Vehicle tires and rubber hoses are made of vulcanized rubber.

Acid rain

Burning fossil fuels releases sulfur and nitrogen compounds into the air. These react with oxygen and water to form acids, which then fall as rain. This acid rain can corrode stone structures, especially statues and buildings made from limestone and marble.

Hot springs in the Danakil Depression, Ethiopia

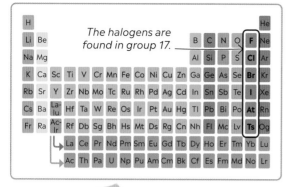

The halogens are found in group 17.

Halogens

The word halogen means "salt forming." Elements in this group form salts when they react with metals. For example, lithium bromide is a compound of the halogen bromine and the metal lithium, while table salt—sodium chloride—is a compound of chlorine and sodium. The first four members of this group—fluorine, chlorine, bromine, and iodine—are all very reactive in nature. Astatine is far less reactive, while the chemistry of tennessine—a halogen confirmed in 2016—is still a mystery.

Cube-shaped crystals

Chlorine

17 Cl

This halogen and its compounds are both dangerous and useful. Pure chlorine gas is toxic and has been used as a weapon, but chemicals known as hypochlorite salts are very effective at killing bacteria in water—making it safe to swim in. Chlorine dioxide is added to water to make sure it is safe to drink.

Common salt

Before it is purified and placed at the dinner table, table salt can be found as a crystalline mineral in its natural form. Known commonly as rock salt, its scientific name is sodium chloride.

This tube shows the level of chlorine in the water. The darker the sample, the more chlorine in the pool.

This tube indicates the pH of the water. The more yellow the sample, the lower the pH value, and the greater the acidity.

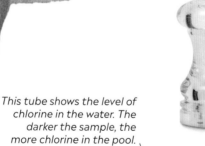

Halite

Chlorine can be extracted from the mineral halite using a process called electrolysis. Dissolving halite in water and passing electricity through it releases chlorine gas. Huge amounts of chlorine can also be found in the ocean.

Purifying water

Chlorine is used to disinfect water in swimming pools. It helps kill bacteria. It's important that the water's acidity is monitored so that the chemicals work effectively. This is measured using the pH scale, which ranges from 0 to 14. A pH of about 7.4–7.6 is ideal.

Fluorine

F 9

The most reactive of all halogens, fluorine has a reputation as a dangerously unstable element. It reacts violently with metals, hydrogen gas, and water and will even react with some noble gases, which are normally inert.

Fluoride

Some fluorine compounds play a vital role in oral health. When added to toothpaste and the water supply in the form of safe fluoride, these compounds help prevent tooth decay by strengthening tooth enamel.

Fluorite

Also known as fluorspar, fluorite is a naturally occurring mineral consisting mainly of the compound calcium fluoride. When fluorite reacts with sulfuric acid, it produces hydrogen fluoride, which is the main source of fluorine in industry.

Fluorite crystals

Green color is due to impurities in the crystal

Deadly pesticide

In the 1940s and 1950s, the chlorine-based chemical DDT (dichloro-diphenyl-trichloroethane) was used widely as a pesticide to curb insect-borne diseases. However, concerns about its impact on wildlife and human health grew until it was banned in the US in 1972. Today, it is banned in most countries and severely restricted in others.

This poster from the 1950s shows an elephant spraying a can of DDT to kill mosquitoes.

These strong pipes—for use in home construction—are composed of PVC.

Indispensable plastic

Arguably one of the most important compounds to contain chlorine is polyvinylchloride (PVC). This type of plastic has a huge number of uses in and around the home, including water pipes, lawn furniture, and waterproof clothing.

Gas warfare

A pungent, yellow-green gas, chlorine affects the eyes, nose, throat, and lungs by causing a choking and irritating effect that can lead to suffocation. Chlorine was first used as a chemical weapon in World War I, which led to the development of gas masks for troops. By World War II, gas masks were provided for troops and civilians alike.

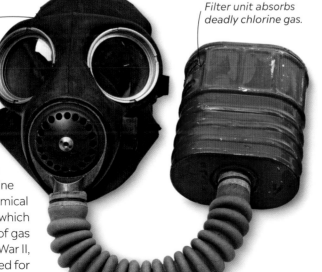

British World War II gas mask

Filter unit absorbs deadly chlorine gas.

Chlorine-based bleach

Bleaching agent

Paper products such as napkins, tissues, and printer paper can be made bright white by using chlorine as a bleaching agent. Household bleach typically contains a chlorine compound called sodium hypochlorite. It destroys germs by breaking down their cell walls.

Bromine

35 Br

The third member of the halogen family, bromine is red-brown and is one of only two elements on the periodic table that are liquid at room temperature, the other being mercury. Toxic in nature, bromine must be handled with care. Its name comes from the Greek word *bromos* meaning "stench"—a reference to its unpleasant smell.

Bromine vapor

A drop of liquid bromine formed at room temperature

Pure bromine stored in a glass sphere

Medicinal salt

Potassium bromide was a key ingredient in the first effective medicines for epilepsy. It was used for human patients until the 1970s, and is still used by vets to control seizures in dogs.

White, salt-like crystals

Bromine purple

Tyrian purple is a naturally occurring dye secreted by some sea snails. It contains a bromine-based compound. In ancient Rome, this dye was highly prized, and purple clothing was seen as a sign of great wealth and importance.

Cloth dyed with Tyrian purple

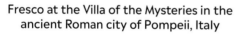

Fresco at the Villa of the Mysteries in the ancient Roman city of Pompeii, Italy

Take a picture

Due to its light sensitivity, silver bromide is used in photography, since film coated with it darkens when exposed to light. This produces a "negative" image, where light areas are dark, and vice versa. This can then be developed into a photograph.

The image darkens on exposure to light.

Muride

Bromine was independently prepared by Carl Jacob Löwig in 1825 and Antoine Jérôme Balard in 1826. Balard extracted it from seawater and named it muride, from *muria*, the Latin word for brine. The French Academy of Science later proposed the name brôme, and in English "ine" was added for consistency with the other halogens.

The Dead Sea in the Middle East contains high quantities of bromine.

Iodine

53 I

The name iodine comes from the Greek word *iodes*, which means "violet." When heated, this halogen changes directly from a solid to a violet vapor without turning into a liquid—a process called sublimation. Iodine is important in our diet because it is vital to the production of chemicals that regulate body functions, including growth.

Iodine vapor

Solid iodine is silvery-gray and its vapor is purple.

Pure iodine stored in a glass sphere

Polarized surface provides extra protection against the sun's ultraviolet radiation.

Seaweed diet

Most seaweed contains a large amount of iodine. The Japanese consume a lot of iodine, as a traditional Japanese diet will often include seaweed.

Protective eyewear

Polarized sunglasses are covered with a thin plastic film dipped in an iodine solution. This coating reduces the sun's harsh glare. Many skiers use polarized glasses because sunlight reflecting off white snow can make it hard to see.

Astatine

85 At

A highly radioactive element, astatine is also rare. A visible sample has never been prepared, because it's so radioactive it would immediately vaporize. It was first isolated in 1940 by Italian-American physicist Emilio Gino Segrè and US physicists Kenneth Ross MacKenzie and Dale R Corson.

Emilio Gino Segrè

In addition to his discovery of astatine, Segrè is also credited with discovering the element technetium. He won the 1959 Nobel Prize in Physics for his discovery of the antiproton—a particle with the same mass as a proton but with a negative electric charge.

Tennessine

117 Ts

In November 2016, element 117 was named tennessine as a tribute to the state of Tennessee. This region is home to the Oak Ridge National Laboratory, which played a prominent role in the research that led to the discovery of this element.

A nuclear reactor at the Oak Ridge National Laboratory, in Tennessee

Researchers use a crane to move fuel rods into the reactor.

Noble Gases

The noble gases sit in group 18—the final group of the periodic table.

Because they are colorless, odorless, tasteless, and mostly unreactive, the noble gases were not easy to identify. But once one was found, the rest followed fairly quickly. Argon was the first of the family to be discovered by the British chemists Morris William Travers and William Ramsay, in 1894. With the subsequent discoveries of helium, krypton, neon, and xenon, a whole new group on the periodic table was established.

This sample of helium is stored in a glass sphere.

Helium

He 2

Although abundant in the universe, helium is not widespread on Earth. The sun and other stars contain a lot of helium, produced by pairs of hydrogen atoms crashing into one another to make helium atoms while releasing massive amounts of energy. On Earth, helium is produced naturally, but very slowly, as a result of radioactive decay.

Helium is a colorless gas, but it glows purple when electrified.

Keeping cool

In a particle accelerator (a machine that smashes atoms together in scientific experiments), liquid helium is injected into the electromagnets to keep the magnets cool. The Large Hadron Collider (LHC) at CERN—the European Organization for Nuclear Research on the French-Swiss border—is the world's biggest particle accelerator

Extreme-helium stars

Unlike most stars that are composed primarily of hydrogen, extreme-helium stars such as Wolf-Rayet 124 (left) are made up of approximately 85 percent helium. Wolf-Rayet 124 is an ultra-massive star surrounded by the intensely hot M1-67 Nebula. This type of star also contains smaller amounts of other elements, including carbon, nitrogen, oxygen, aluminum, iron, chromium, and nickel.

Wolf-Rayet 124 glows inside the M1-67 Nebula.

Neon

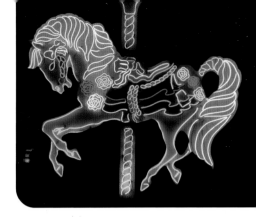

10 Ne Perhaps the most well known of all noble gases for its role in neon signs, neon is an unreactive element. Like helium, this transparent gas is commonly found throughout the universe but is rare on Earth. Unlike helium, which is found mixed in natural gas, neon is available only in air. It is extracted by cooling air until it becomes a liquid. In industry, neon is used as a coolant as well as in making some types of fluorescent lamps and in diving equipment.

This sample of neon is stored in a glass sphere. Normally a colorless gas, it gives off a red-orange glow when electrified.

Neon lights

Gas tubes filled with neon are commonly used in bright red signs and lights. Although they are all called "neon lights," the other colors are not actually neon, but other elements—for example, helium (yellow), argon (purple), and mercury (blue).

A helium–neon laser beam appears red in color.

Weather balloons collect wind data, including temperature and speed, as well as atmospheric pressure readings at high altitudes.

Scanning codes

Bar codes store data about a product that can only be read by machines. Some bar code scanners use lasers made of a combination of helium and neon. These efficient lasers use very little energy and are used in supermarkets and retail shops throughout the world.

Up, up, and away

Helium has been used in all types of balloons, including weather balloons and party balloons. Since helium gas is lighter than air, balloons filled with it float upward. Unlike hydrogen, helium is not flammable, making it a much safer choice.

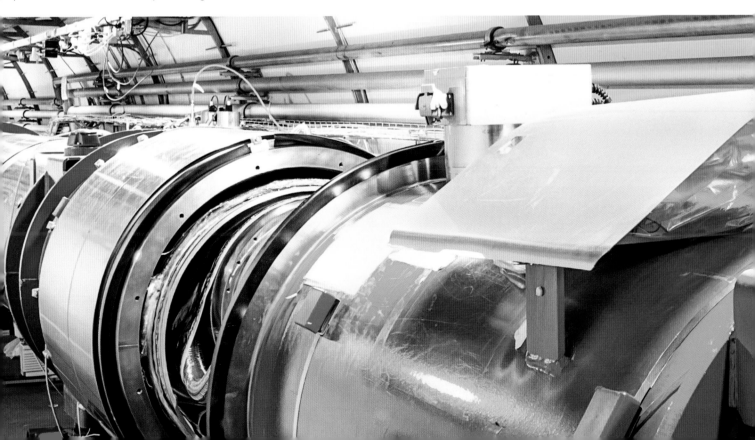

Argon

Ar 18

This element's name comes from *argos*, the Greek word for "idle." True to its name, this gas almost never reacts with other elements, although scientists have managed to produce a compound of hydrogen, fluorine, and argon. Because it's fairly plentiful—making up about 1 percent of Earth's atmosphere—it's often used in food packaging, where it stops food from spoiling.

Argon gives off a blue-purple color when it is electrified.

Pure argon in a glass sphere

Fighting fire

Argon extinguishers are recommended for suppressing electrical fires. The gas does not damage expensive equipment by leaving a residue, making it a popular choice for fire extinguishers in server and data rooms, museums, archives, and laboratories.

ARGON
UN 1006
NET WEIGHT
25 KG

FOR INDUSTRIAL USE ONLY

The blue argon laser targets the retina during eye surgery.

Non-invasive surgery

Laser surgical procedures do not make incisions, and, consequently, the affected area heals quickly. In the case of eye surgery, this blue argon laser can be used for a wide range of delicate operations on the retina.

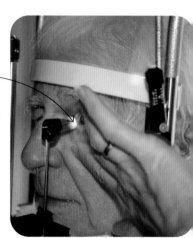

Krypton

Kr 36

A colorless, odorless gas, krypton means "the hidden one" in Greek. It plays an important role in airport safety, as the flashing lights on most modern airport runways are filled with this gas, giving off very bright light. It is more reactive than the other noble gases—reacting with fluorine to produce krypton fluoride.

Krypton-powered airport runway lights

Oganesson

Og 118

Only a few atoms of this highly radioactive element have been made in a laboratory. As such, not much is known about it. Although oganesson falls into group 18 with the noble gases, scientists think it could be more reactive, and might be a solid at room temperature. Discovered by a group of Russian and American scientists in Dubna, Russia, the element is named after Yuri Oganessian, the leader of the team.

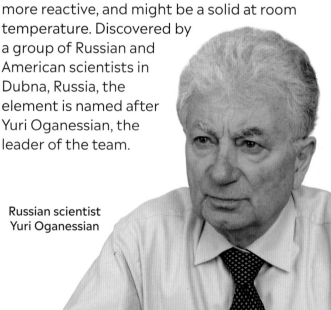

Russian scientist Yuri Oganessian

Xenon

54 Xe Like most members of its group, xenon is also an unreactive, colorless, and odorless element. However, it glows a striking blue when a high voltage is applied to it, and this property makes it a valuable component in car headlights and studio lights. Some rocket engines use xenon-based thrusters to propel the spacecraft forward.

Pure xenon electrified in a glass sphere

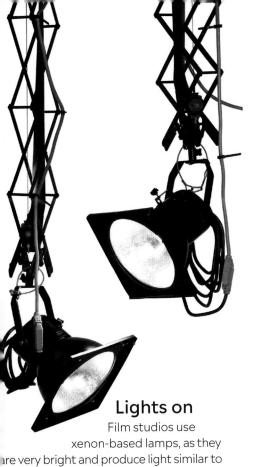

Lights on

Film studios use xenon-based lamps, as they are very bright and produce light similar to natural sunlight. Special effects artists use this type of light source to create an intense, straight beam of light on film sets.

The Dawn *spacecraft carried 937 lb (425 kg) of xenon at launch.*

Rocket fuel

Xenon is used as a propellant in some rocket engines. Chemically inert and easily stored in a compact form, its atoms are heavy, so they provide more thrust compared to other propellants.

Artist's impression of NASA's *Dawn* spacecraft

Radon

86 Rn Produced by the breakdown of uranium and other radioactive elements, radon is the only natural radioactive noble gas. In most places, this element is only present in tiny amounts, yet it is still responsible for most of the radiation on Earth. As radon moves up through the ground it can accumulate in buildings. This can become harmful, so it's important that its levels are checked and monitored.

Radioactive materials in this mineral break down to emit radon gas.

Uraninite

Glass sphere containing radon and air

The water from this volcanic hot spring contains radon.

Hot spring baths

Radon escapes from volcanic hot springs and muds along with other gases, such as carbon dioxide and sulfur dioxide. While radon is considered to be toxic by environmental agencies, some health-seekers visit thermal baths for a dip in these waters.

Glossary

ACID A corrosive substance that will react with a base (see base) to form a salt and water.

ALCHEMY Practices in medieval times that tried to turn common metals, such as lead, into gold.

ALKALI A soluble base (see base).

ALLOY A mixture of two or more metals.

ATMOSPHERIC PRESSURE The pressure created by the gases surrounding Earth.

ATOM The smallest unit of an element.

ATOMIC MASS The mass of an atom measured in atomic mass units (AMU).

BASE A corrosive substance that will react with an acid to form a salt and water.

BLOCK Larger sets of elements on the periodic table, which may have similar properties.

BOND The attraction between atoms or ions that holds them together in an element or a compound.

Saxophone made of bronze, a copper-tin alloy

CATALYST A substance that can be added to a chemical reaction to speed it up.

COMBUSTION A chemical reaction in which a fuel burns in the presence of oxygen.

COMPOUND A substance made up of elements bonded together.

CONDUCTIVITY The ability of a substance to let electricity, sound, or heat pass through it.

CORROSION The process of a metal breaking down by chemically reacting with substances in the environment. An example of this is the rusting of iron through reactions with oxygen and water.

CYCLOTRON A type of particle accelerator. Particle accelerators are machines used to smash atoms into one another at incredibly high speeds.

ELECTROLYSIS A technique that uses electricity to break salt compounds down into simpler substances.

ELECTRON A negatively charged particle that orbits the nucleus of an atom.

ELEMENT A substance that cannot be broken down into anything simpler.

EMISSION The process of giving off light, heat, radiation, or particles.

FISSION The process of splitting the nucleus of an atom into smaller fragments.

FOSSIL FUEL A substance formed in Earth's crust from the remains of ancient organisms. Humans use this as fuel.

FUEL CELL A device that converts chemical energy into electricity.

FUSION Where two or more atomic nuclei combine to form different atomic nuclei.

GALVANIZATION The process of electrically coating steel with zinc to protect it from corrosion.

GENETICS The study of inherited traits between different organisms.

GROUP A vertical column of elements on the periodic table, with elements that often have similar properties.

HALF-LIFE The time taken for half of the nuclei in a radioactive sample to undergo decay (see nuclear decay).

INERT A way of describing a substance that does not easily undergo a chemical reaction.

INSULATOR A substance that does not let electricity, sound, or heat flow through it easily.

ION A charged particle produced when an atom either loses or gains electrons.

ISOTOPE A form of an element with atoms that have the same number of protons but a different number of neutrons.

MALLEABILITY A metal's ability to be reshaped.

MELTING POINT The temperature at which a solid gets hot enough to turn into a liquid.

METAL An element that is usually found as a shiny solid and is a good conductor of electricity and heat.

Crystals of the element bismuth

METALLOID An element that displays properties of both metals and non-metals.

MINERAL A naturally occurring form of a chemical compound, usually found in Earth's crust.

MOLECULE A group of atoms that are chemically bonded to one another.

NEUTRON A neutral subatomic particle found in the nucleus of an atom.

NUCLEAR BOMB An explosive device that releases large amounts of energy and can cause mass devastation.

NUCLEAR DECAY A natural process in which the nuclei of radioactive atoms break down or rearrange themselves to form new nuclei.

NUCLEAR REACTOR A device used to carry out a controlled nuclear reaction.

Rust on motorcycle, an example of corrosion

NUCLEUS The dense center of an atom where protons and neutrons are found.

OPTICAL CLOCK A special type of clock that uses light and single atoms to keep highly accurate time.

ORBITAL Spherical layer, or shell, around the nucleus of an atom where electrons can be found.

ORE Naturally occurring rock from which useful minerals can be extracted.

ORGANIC CHEMISTRY A branch of chemistry that deals with the chemistry of carbon and its compounds.

OXIDE A compound that forms when an element combines with oxygen.

PERIOD A horizontal row of elements on the periodic table, with elements that often have very different properties.

PH SCALE A numerical scale used to describe the acidic or basic properties of a substance. Less than 7 on the scale is described as acidic, above 7 as basic, and 7 as neutral.

Pellets of radioactive californium

PHOTOSYNTHESIS Naturally occurring chemical reaction that plants use to turn light energy into chemical energy.

Fluorite, a mineral containing fluorine

POROUS A material with tiny holes through which liquids can pass.

PROTON A positively charged particle in the nucleus of an atom.

RADIATION Energy released, usually in the form of waves or particles.

RADIOACTIVITY A process that occurs when an atom is unstable because the protons and neutrons in the nucleus do not stick together.

REACTIVITY A substance's tendency to undergo chemical reactions.

SALT A compound that forms when an acid reacts with an alkali. Sodium chloride is the most familiar example of a salt.

SEMICONDUCTOR A material that conducts electricity better than an insulator but not as well as a metal.

SOLUBLE A substance that dissolves in a solvent (usually water).

STATES OF MATTER The three common states of matter are solid, liquid, or gas. In solids, particles are bound to each other, so they remain in fixed positions. In liquids, particles are loosely attached to each other and move freely. In gases, particles are not attached to each other and can move away.

SUBATOMIC PARTICLE A particle that makes up an atom. These include protons, neutrons, and electrons.

SUPERALLOY A combination of metals that can withstand extreme temperature and pressure.

SUPER-HEAVY ELEMENTS Elements with the atomic number 104 or higher.

SYNTHETIC ELEMENT An element created artificially in a laboratory.

TEMPERATURE How hot or cold something is as measured on a defined scale.

TOXICITY A measure of the poisonous properties of a substance.

TRANSURANIUM ELEMENTS Elements with an atomic number higher than that of uranium (92).

ULTRAVIOLET RAYS Invisible electromagnetic radiation with very short wavelengths. It is called ultraviolet because it is beyond the violet end of visible light on the electromagnetic spectrum.

Jet engine with inner blades made of a rhenium superalloy

VAPOR A mixture of gaseous and liquid particles of a substance suspended in air.

VERDIGRIS A gray-green layer that forms on copper when it is exposed to air.

VOLTAGE The force that pushes an electrical current around a circuit.

X-RAY A type of powerful electromagnetic radiation. X-rays can pass right through human tissue but not bone and are used in medical science to take internal pictures of the human body.

Index

Acknowledgments

The publisher would like to thank the following people with their help with making the book:
Srestha Bhattacharya and Neha Ruth Samuel for editorial assistance; Aparajita Sen for design assistance;
Jo Penning for the index; and Hazel Beynon for proofreading.

The publisher would like to thank the following for their kind permission to reproduce their photographs:
(Key: a-above; b-below/bottom; c-centre; f-far; l-left; r-right; t-top)

1 Dorling Kindersley: Ruth Jenkinson / RGB Research Limited. **2 123RF.com:** David Barnard (clb). **Dorling Kindersley:** Ruth Jenkinson / RGB Research Limited (tl, bl, cra). **Dreamstime.com:** Yehuda Bernstein (tr). **Getty Images:** Viviane Ponti (br). **4 Alamy Stock Photo:** The Granger Collection (tr). **Dorling Kindersley:** Ruth Jenkinson / RGB Research Limited (clb, br). **5 Dorling Kindersley:** Ruth Jenkinson / RGB Research Limited (bl). **7 123RF.com:** Kubais (br). **Alamy Stock Photo:** Science History Images (tc). **9 Alamy Stock Photo:** The Granger Collection (bc). **10 Dorling Kindersley:** Ruth Jenkinson / RGB Research Limited (cl, c, cr, bl, bc, br). **11 Dorling Kindersley:** Ruth Jenkinson / RGB Research Limited (cla, ca, cd, bl, bc, br). **12-13 123RF.com:** Reinhold Wittich (cr). **12 123RF.com:** Utima (clb). **Dorling Kindersley:** Ruth Jenkinson / RGB Research Limited (cl). **Getty Images:** Gamma-Rapho / Tatsuyuki TAYAMA (cra). **14 123RF.com:** Ramon Espelt Gorgozo (br). **Dorling Kindersley:** Ruth Jenkinson / RGB Research Limited (cl). **15 Dreamstime.com:** Gnomeandi (br). **Dorling Kindersley:** Ruth Jenkinson / RGB Research Limited (cl). **16 123RF.com:** Belchonock (cl); karandaev (fcl); Kostic Dusan (bl). **Alamy Stock Photo:** Siim Sepp (ca). **Dorling Kindersley:** Ruth Jenkinson / RGB Research Limited (tc). **500px** / Marc Lapointe (crb). **17 Alamy Stock Photo:** David Leone Ganado (tr); Newscom (bc). **Dorling Kindersley:** Ruth Jenkinson / RGB Research Limited (cla, clb, br). **18 Dorling Kindersley:** Ruth Jenkinson / Holts Gems (cl). **NASA:** MSFC / David Higginbotham (br). **19 123RF.com:** Georgios Kollidas (bl); Sergii Popov (bc). **Dorling Kindersley:** Ruth Jenkinson / RGB Research Limited (cla). **Science Photo Library:** GIPhotoStock (cr). **20 123RF.com:** Steve Carroll (cr); Ben Gingell (bl). **Dorling Kindersley:** Ruth Jenkinson / RGB Research Limited (cl). **Dreamstime.com:** Yehuda Bernstein (t). **21 Alamy Stock Photo:** US Marines Photo (cl). **Dorling Kindersley:** Ruth Jenkinson / RGB Research Limited (cla). **Getty Images:** Print Collector / Oxford Science Archive (br). **Science Photo Library:** Biophoto Associates (cra); J C Revy (bc). **22 Alamy Stock Photo:** Shooterstack (cra). **Dorling Kindersley:** Ruth Jenkinson / RGB Research Limited (bd). **Getty Images:** Barcroft Media / Jefta Images (br). **23 123RF.com:** Hapelena (tr). **Alamy Stock Photo:** Oleksiy Maksymenko (br). **Dorling Kindersley:** Ruth Jenkinson / RGB Research Limited (cla). **500px** / Maciej Sznek (tr). **24 123RF.com:** Ruslan Gilmanshin (cr). **Dorling Kindersley:** Ruth Jenkinson / RGB Research Limited (cla). **Dreamstime.com:** Nexus7 (cra). **Getty Images:** Viviane Ponti (br). **Rex Shutterstock:** Glasshouse Images (tc). **25 Alamy Stock Photo:** H.S. Photos (ca); Margo Harrison (cra). **Dorling Kindersley:** Ruth Jenkinson / RGB Research Limited (crb). **Dreamstime.com:** Radlovskyaroslav (br). **FLPA:** Biosphoto / Nicolas-Alain Petit (bl, clb). **26 123RF.com:** David Barnard (cla); Koosen (bl); Sandra van der Steen (cra); Chris Elwell (bc). **Dorling Kindersley:** Ruth Jenkinson / RGB Research Limited (tc, crb). **Dreamstime.com:** Stockshooter (cra). **27 Alamy Stock Photo:** Susan E. Degginger (bl). **Dorling Kindersley:** Ruth Jenkinson / RGB Research Limited (tc, tr); Gary Ombler / The Tank Museum, Bovington (cr). **SuperStock:** Age fotostock / Humbert (ca); Age fotostock / Phil Robinson (cra). **28 123RF.com:** Nerthuz (ca). **Dorling Kindersley:** Ruth Jenkinson / RGB Research Limited (tc, bl, crb). **Practicon** www.practicon.com (br). **29 Dakota Matrix Minerals, photo by Tom Loomis** (cla). **Dorling Kindersley:** Ruth Jenkinson / RGB Research Limited (tl, cb). **Getty Images:** Deniztuyel (bl). **Science Photo Library:** (cra). **30 Alamy Stock Photo:** Ableimages (cla); Dembinsky Photo Associates / Mark A Schneider (tr). **Dorling Kindersley:** Ruth Jenkinson / RGB Research Limited (ca, cb, cla). **31 123RF.com:** Mishoo (tr); Anton Starikov (tl). **Dorling Kindersley:** Ruth Jenkinson / RGB Research Limited (cb). **Getty Images:** De Agostini / DEA / R. Appiani (cla). **© Rolls-Royce plc:** (bc). **Science Photo Library:** Detlev van Ravenswaay (br); Dirk Wiersma (cra). **32 Dorling Kindersley:** Ruth Jenkinson / RGB Research Limited (br); Natural History Museum, London / Tim Parmenter (tl). **Dreamstime.com:** Maloy40 (ca). **Science Photo Library:** Gary Brown (tr). **33 Dorling Kindersley:** Ruth Jenkinson / RGB Research Limited (tc). **Getty Images:** Alison Wright (b). **NASA:** (cl). **Numismatica Ars Classica NAC AG:** Auction 59, lot 658 (c). **34 Alamy Stock Photo:** Science History Images (cla). **Getty Images:** Bettmann (bl). **Lawrence Berkeley National Laboratory:** © 2010 The Regents of the University of California (cra). **35 Alamy Stock Photo:** DPA Picture Alliance Archive (cr); Mieczyslaw Wieliczko (br). **Getty Images:** Bettmann (br). **Science Photo Library:** Emilio Segre Visual Archives / American Institute Of Physics (cra). **36 Alamy Stock Photo:** John Cancalosi (cra). **Dorling Kindersley:** Ruth Jenkinson / RGB Research Limited (c, br). **Science Photo Library. 37 Michael Brandon:** (cra). **Dorling Kindersley:** Ruth Jenkinson / RGB Research Limited (tl, tr, br). **Science Photo Library. 38 Alamy Stock Photo:** PjrStudio (br).

Dorling Kindersley: Ruth Jenkinson / RGB Research Limited (tc). **Getty Images:** Spaces Images (bl). **Science Photo Library:** Zephyr (ca). **39 Dorling Kindersley:** Ruth Jenkinson / RGB Research Limited (cb, cr). **Rex Shutterstock:** Shutterstock / Mint Images (cla). **Science Photo Library. 40 Alamy Stock Photo:** John Cancalosi (cra). **Science Photo Library:** Public Health England (crb). **41 Alamy Stock Photo:** Natural History Museum (tr); PF-(bygone1) (cla); Sciencephotos (br). **Dorling Kindersley:** Ruth Jenkinson / RGB Research Limited (bl). **Getty Images:** Bettmann (crb). **42 123RF.com:** Victor Bouchard (bl). **Dorling Kindersley:** Ruth Jenkinson / RGB Research Limited (cb). **Science Photo Library:** Ned Haines (cl). **42-43 Alamy Stock Photo:** Science History Images. **43 Getty Images:** Walter Bibikow (cr); Scientifica (tr). **Science Photo Library:** Detlev van Ravenswaay (br). **44 Alamy Stock Photo:** Ewing Galloway (cl); Keystone Pictures USA (b). **US Department of Energy:** (cr). **45 Alamy Stock Photo:** Akademie (c); Everett Collection Historical (tl); Heritage Image Partnership Ltd (bl); Science History Images (cr). **46-47 123RF.com:** Senohrabek (b). **46 Alamy Stock Photo:** Phil Degginger (bl). **Dorling Kindersley:** Ruth Jenkinson / RGB Research Limited (cla, cr). **Getty Images:** Bettmann (crb). **47 123RF.com:** Fullempty (tr); Bogdan Ionescu (cla); Winterstorm (cl); Roman Samokhin (cb). **Alamy Stock Photo:** Simon Belcher (cr). **Dorling Kindersley:** Ruth Jenkinson / RGB Research Limited (bl, cr, tc). **Getty Images:** John B. Carnett (c). **49 123RF.com:** Ratchanida Thippayos (ca). **Dorling Kindersley:** Ruth Jenkinson / RGB Research Limited (bl, cr, tc). **Getty Images:** The Asahi Shimbun (br). **50 Alamy Stock Photo:** Oleksiy (cr). **Dorling Kindersley:** Ruth Jenkinson / RGB Research Limited (cb). **Getty Images:** Dimitri Otis (ca). **Science Photo Library:** James King-Holmes (bl). **50-51 Alamy Stock Photo:** Palmer Photographics (b). **51 123RF.com:** Aleksey Poprugin (c); Anton Starikov (cla). **Depositphotos Inc:** Crstrbrt (tr). **Getty Images:** Hans-Peter Merten (cr). **iStockphoto.com:** Kerrick (cl). **52 Alamy Stock Photo:** NPC Collection (cla); Sputnik (tr); Traveler (tr). **Dorling Kindersley:** Ruth Jenkinson / RGB Research Limited (tc, cb). **Rice University:** Jeff Fitlow (bl). **53 123RF.com:** James Blinn (br); mipan (bc). **Dorling Kindersley:** Ruth Jenkinson / RGB Research Limited (cla); Dave King / Durham University Oriental Museum (cl). **54 Dorling Kindersley:** Ruth Jenkinson / RGB Research Limited (br). **54-55 Alamy Stock Photo:** Ernie Janes (b). **55 123RF.com:** Ayphoto (cra). **Alamy Stock Photo:** Robert Clayton (br). **56 Alamy Stock Photo:** Science History Images (b). **Getty Images:** Morley Read (l). **57 123RF.com:** Aleksandar Mijatovic (cb). **Alamy Stock Photo:** Pictorial Press Ltd (cra). **Dorling Kindersley:** Ruth Jenkinson / RGB Research Limited (cla, bl). **Getty Images:** Universal History Archive (cla). **58 123RF.com:** Wavebreak Media Ltd (crb). **Dorling Kindersley:** Ruth Jenkinson / RGB Research Limited (cl). **Getty Images:** Georgette Douwma (bl). **59 123RF.com:** sin32 (r). **Alamy Stock Photo:** Falkensteinfoto (cb); Image Source (c). **Getty Images:** Harry Kikstra (tl). **60 Dorling Kindersley:** Ruth Jenkinson / RGB Research Limited (cla, bl, cra). **Photo James D. Julia Auctioneers, Fairfield, Maine, USA** www.jamesdjulia.com: Lamp by Charles Lotton "Multi Flora" 1993 (cr). **60-61 Getty Images:** Barcroft Media / Massimo Rumi (b). **61 123RF.com:** photo5963 (clb). **Getty Images:** Photofusion (cb). **62 Alamy Stock Photo:** Brian Elliott (bc). **63 123RF.com:** Hieng Ling Tie (ca). **Alamy Stock Photo:** Paris Pierce (cl). **Dorling Kindersley:** Wardrobe Museum, Salisbury / Gary Ombler (br). **Getty Images:** Andy Sotiriou (cr). **64 123RF.com:** Sean Pavone (b). **Alamy Stock Photo:** I. Glory (cr). **Dorling Kindersley:** Ruth Jenkinson / RGB Research Limited (cla, cl). **Getty Images:** Soltan Frédéric (r). **65 123RF.com:** Sergey Mironov (cra). **Dorling Kindersley:** Ruth Jenkinson / RGB Research Limited (tc). **Dreamstime.com:** Daniel Poloha / Spidermom (cla). **Science Photo Library:** Keystone (bc). **Science Photo Library:** Union Carbide Corporation's Nuclear Division, courtesy Emilio Segre Visual Archives, Physics Today Collection / American Institute of Physics (cr). **66-67 iStockphoto.com:** (b). **66 Dorling Kindersley:** Ruth Jenkinson / RGB Research Limited (cl). **ESA:** Hubble & NASA Processed by Judy Schmidt (bl). **67 123RF.com:** (cl). **Alamy Stock Photo:** Keith Morris (cr). **Dorling Kindersley:** Ruth Jenkinson / RGB Research Limited (tl). **500px** / Henry Buchholtz (tr). **68 123RF.com:** Scanrail (ca). **Alamy Stock Photo:** Roger Bamber (br); ITAR-TASS Photo Agency (br). **Dorling Kindersley:** Ruth Jenkinson / RGB Research Limited (tr). **Science Photo Library:** Antonia Reeve (cra). **69 Alamy Stock Photo:** Gordon Mills (bl); Prill Mediendesign (tl). **Dorling Kindersley:** Ruth Jenkinson / RGB Research Limited (tr, br). **NASA:** Christopher J. Lynch (Wyle Information Systems, LLC) (ca). **Science Photo Library:** Dirk Wiersma (cra). **70-71 123RF.com:** Sean Pavone (b). **Dorling Kindersley:** Ruth Jenkinson / RGB Research Limited (c). **70 123RF.com:** Ruslan Gilmanshin (b); Sandra van der Steen (ca). **71 © Rolls-Royce plc:** (cr). **US Department of Energy:** (bc)

All other images © Dorling Kindersley

For further information see: **www.dkimages.com**

WHAT WILL YOU EYEWITNESS NEXT?

Packed with pictures and full of facts, DK Eyewitness books are perfect for school projects and home learning.

AMERICAN REVOLUTION

ANCIENT EGYPT

ANCIENT ROME

CAT

CLIMATE CHANGE

DINOSAUR

FISH

HURRICANE & TORNADO

NATURAL DISASTERS

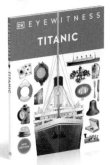
OCEAN

ROCKS & MINERALS

SHARK

THE AMAZON

THE ELEMENTS

TITANIC

TRAIN

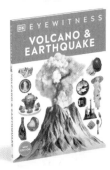
VOLCANO & EARTHQUAKE

WEATHER

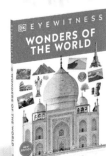
WONDERS OF THE WORLD

WORLD WAR II

Also available:

Eyewitness Amphibian
Eyewitness Ancient China
Eyewitness Ancient Civilizations
Eyewitness Ancient Greece
Eyewitness Animal
Eyewitness Arms and Armor
Eyewitness Astronomy
Eyewitness Aztec, Inca & Maya
Eyewitness Baseball
Eyewitness Bible Lands
Eyewitness Bird
Eyewitness Car
Eyewitness Castle

Eyewitness Chemistry
Eyewitness Crystals & Gems
Eyewitness Dog
Eyewitness Early People
Eyewitness Eagle and Birds of Prey
Eyewitness Electricity
Eyewitness Endangered Animals
Eyewitness Energy
Eyewitness Flight
Eyewitness Forensic Science
Eyewitness Fossil
Eyewitness Great Scientists
Eyewitness Horse

Eyewitness Human Body
Eyewitness Insect
Eyewitness Judaism
Eyewitness Knight
Eyewitness Medieval Life
Eyewitness Mesopotamia
Eyewitness Money
Eyewitness Mummy
Eyewitness Mythology
Eyewitness National Parks
Eyewitness North American Indian
Eyewitness Plant
Eyewitness Planets
Eyewitness Prehistoric Life

Eyewitness Presidents
Eyewitness Religion
Eyewitness Reptile
Eyewitness Robot
Eyewitness Shakespeare
Eyewitness Soccer
Eyewitness Soldier
Eyewitness Space Exploration
Eyewitness The Civil War
Eyewitness Tree
Eyewitness Universe
Eyewitness Vietnam War
Eyewitness Viking
Eyewitness World War I

DK For the curious